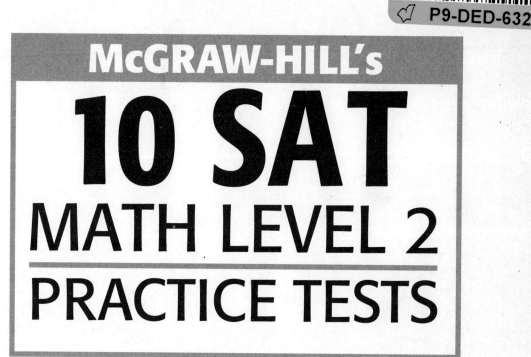

McGRAW-HILL's
10 SAT
MATH LEVEL 2
PRACTICE TESTS

McGRAW-HILL's

10 SAT
MATH LEVEL 2
PRACTICE TESTS

Christine Caputo

New York / Chicago / San Francisco / Lisbon / London / Madrid / Mexico City
Milan / New Delhi / San Juan / Seoul / Singapore / Sydney / Toronto

2051 5528 7

1 2 3 4 5 6 7 8 9 10   QDB/QDB   1 9 8 7 6 5 4 3 1

ISBN 978-0-07-176292-2
MHID 0-07-176292-2

e-ISBN 978-0-07-176293-9
e-MHID 0-07-176293-0

Library of Congress Control Number: 2011914994

McGraw-Hill books are available at special quantity discounts to use as premiums and sales promotions or for use in corporate training programs. To contact a representative, please e-mail us at bulksales@ mcgraw-hill.com.

SAT is a registered trademark of the College Entrance Examination Board, which was not involved in the production of, and does not endorse, this product.

CONTENTS

McGRAW-HILL's
10 SAT
MATH LEVEL 2
PRACTICE TESTS

PART I
ABOUT THE SAT MATH LEVEL 2 TEST

CHAPTER 1
TEST BASICS

ABOUT THE MATH LEVEL 2 TEST

The SAT Math Level 2 test is one of the Subject Tests offered by the College Board. It tests your knowledge of high school math concepts and differs from the SAT, which tests your math *aptitude*. The test consists of 50 multiple-choice questions and is one hour long.

The SAT Subject Tests (formerly known as the SAT II tests or Achievement Tests) are the lesser-known counterpart to the SAT, offered by the same organization—the College Board. However, whereas the SAT tests general verbal, writing, and mathematical reasoning skills, the SAT Subject Tests cover specific knowledge in a wide variety of subjects, including English, Mathematics, History, Science, and Foreign Languages. SAT Subject Tests are only one hour long, significantly shorter than the SAT, and you can take up to three tests during any one test administration day. You can choose which SAT Subject Tests to take and how many to take on one test day, but you cannot register for both the SAT and Subject Tests on the same test day.

The Math Level 2 test covers the topics shown in the pie chart below.

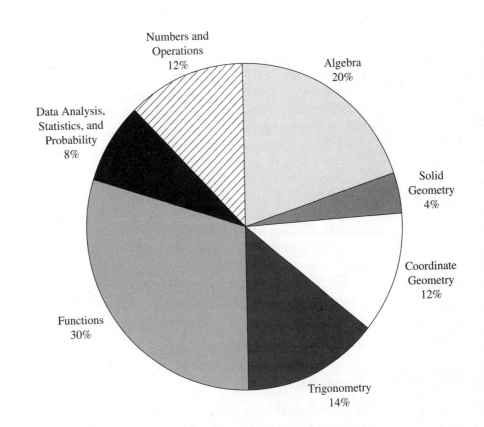

The Math Level 2 test is designed to test a student's math knowledge, ability to apply concepts, and higher-order thinking. Students are not expected to know every topic covered on the test.

When determining which SAT Subject Tests to take and when to take them, consult your high school guidance counselor and pick up a copy of the "Taking the SAT Subject Tests" bulletin published by the College Board. Research the admissions policies of colleges to which you are considering applying to determine their SAT Subject Test requirements and the average scores students receive. Also, visit the College Board's website at www.collegeboard.com to learn more about what tests are offered.

Use this book to become familiar with the content, organization, and level of difficulty of the Math Level 2 test. Knowing what to expect on the day of the test will allow you to do your best.

WHEN TO TAKE THE TEST

The Math Level 2 test is recommended for students who have completed *more than* 3 years of college-preparatory mathematics. Most students taking the Level 2 test have studied 2 years of algebra, 1 year of geometry, and 1 year of precalculus (elementary functions) and/or trigonometry. Many students take the math Subject Tests at the end of their junior year or at the beginning of their senior year.

Colleges look at SAT Subject Test scores to see a student's academic achievement because the test results are less subjective than other parts of a college application, such as GPA, teacher recommendations, student background information, and the interview. Many colleges require at least one SAT Subject Test score for admission, but even schools that do not require SAT Subject Tests may review your scores to get an overall picture of your qualifications. Colleges may also use SAT Subject Test scores to enroll students in appropriate courses. If math is your strongest subject, then a high SAT Math score, combined with good grades on your transcript, can convey that strength to a college or university.

To register for SAT Subject Tests, pick up a copy of the Registration Bulletin, "Registering for the SAT: SAT Reasoning Test, SAT Subject Tests" from your guidance counselor. You can also register at www.collegeboard.com or contact the College Board directly by mail.

General inquiries can be directed via email through the Web site's email inquiry form or by telephone.

The SAT Math Level 2 test is administered six Saturdays (or Sunday if you qualify because of religious beliefs) a year in October, November, December, January, May, and June. Students may take up to three SAT Subject Tests per test day.

THE LEVEL 1 VS. LEVEL 2 TEST

As mentioned, the Math Level 2 test is recommended for students who have completed *more than* 3 years of college-preparatory mathematics. The Math Level 1 test is recommended for students who have completed 3 years of college-preparatory mathematics. Most students taking the Level 1 test have studied 2 years of algebra and 1 year of geometry.

Typically, students who have received A or B grades in precalculus and trigonometry elect to take the Level 2 test. If you have taken more than 3 years of high school math and are enrolled in a precalculus or calculus program, don't assume that taking the Level 1 test guarantees a higher score. Many of the topics on the Level 1 test will be concepts you studied years ago.

Although the topics covered on the two tests overlap somewhat, they differ as shown in the table below. The College Board gives an approximate outline of the mathematics covered on each test as follows:

Topic	Level 1 Test	Level 2 Test
Algebra and Functions	38–42%	48–52%
Plane Euclidean Geometry	18–22%	—
Three-dimensional Geometry	4–6%	4–6%
Coordinate Geometry	8–12%	10–14%
Trigonometry	6–8%	12–16%
Data Analysis, Statistics, and Probability	8–12%	8–12%
Number and Operations	10–14%	10–14%

Overall, the Level 2 test focuses on more advanced content in each area. As shown in the table, the Level 2 test does not directly cover Plane Euclidean Geometry, although Plane Euclidean Geometry concepts may be applied in other types of questions. Number and Operations was formerly known as Miscellaneous.

This book provides a detailed review of all the areas covered on the Math Level 2 test. More advanced topics that are covered only on the Level 2 test are denoted by an asterisk (*) in the topics list at the beginning of each of the math review chapters.

SCORING

The scoring of the Math Level 2 test is based on a 200–800-point scale, similar to that of the math and verbal sections of the SAT. You receive one point for each correct answer and lose one quarter of a point for each incorrect answer. You do not lose any points for omitting a question. In addition to your scaled score, your score report shows a percentile ranking indicating the percentage of students scoring below your score. Because there are considerable differences between the Math Level 1 and Level 2 tests, your score on one is not an accurate indicator of your score on the other.

Score reports are mailed, at no charge, approximately 5 weeks after the test day. Score reports are available approximately 3 weeks after the test day for free at www.collegeboard.com. Just as with the SAT, you can choose up to four college/scholarship program codes to which to send your scores, and the College Board will send a cumulative report of all of your SAT and SAT Subject Test scores to these programs. Additional score reports can be requested, for a fee, online or by telephone.

HOW TO USE THIS BOOK

- **Identify the subject matter that you need to review.** Complete the first test and evaluate your score. Identify your areas of weakness and focus your test preparation on these areas.
- **Practice your test-taking skills and pacing.** Complete the practice tests under actual test-like conditions. Evaluate your scores on each test, and again, review your areas of weakness.

CHAPTER 2

CALCULATOR TIPS

The SAT Math Level 2 test requires the use of a scientific or graphing calculator. The Math Level 1 and Level 2 tests are actually the only Subject Tests for which calculators are allowed. It is not necessary to use a calculator to solve every problem on the test. In fact, there is no advantage to using a calculator for 35–45% of the Level 2 test questions. That means a calculator is helpful for solving approximately 55–65% of the Level 2 test questions.

It is critical to know how and when to use your calculator effectively, and how and when to NOT use your calculator. For some problems, using a calculator may actually take longer than solving the problem by hand. Knowing how to operate your calculator properly will affect your test score, so practice using your calculator when completing the practice tests in this book.

The Level 2 test is created with the understanding that most students know how to use a graphing calculator. Although you have a choice of using either a scientific or a graphing calculator, **choose a graphing calculator.** A graphing calculator provides much more functionality (as long as you know how to use it properly!). A graphing calculator is an advantage when solving many problems related to coordinate geometry and functions.

Remember to make sure your calculator is working properly before your test day. Become comfortable with using it and familiar with the common operations. Because calculator policies are ever changing, refer to www. collegeboard.com for the latest information. According to the College Board, the following types of calculators are NOT allowed on the test:

- calculators with QWERTY (typewriter-like) keypads
- calculators that contain electronic dictionaries
- calculators with paper tape or printers
- calculators that "talk" or make noise
- calculators that require an electrical outlet
- cell-phone calculators
- pocket organizers or personal digital assistants
- hand-held minicomputers, powerbooks, or laptop computers
- electronic writing pads or pen-input/stylus-driven devices (such as a Palm Pilot)

There are a few rules to calculator usage on the SAT Subject Tests. Of course, you may not share your calculator with another student during the test. Doing so may result in dismissal from the test. If your calculator has a large or raised display that can be seen by other test takers, the test supervisor has the right to assign you to an appropriate seat, presumably not in the line of sight of other students. Calculators may not be on your desk during other SAT Subject Tests, aside from the Math Level 1 and Level 2 tests. If your calculator malfunctions during the test, and you don't have a backup or extra batteries, you can either choose to continue the test without a calculator or choose to cancel your test score. You must cancel the score before leaving the test center. If you leave the test center, you must cancel your scores for all Subject Tests taken on that date.

When choosing what calculator to use for the test make sure your calculator performs the following functions:

- squaring a number
- raising a number to a power other than 2 (usually the {^} button)
- taking the square root of a number
- taking the cube root of a number (or, in other words, raising a number to the $\frac{1}{3}$ power)
- sine, cosine, and tangent
- $\sin^{-1}$, $\cos^{-1}$, $\tan^{-1}$
- can be set to both degree mode and radian mode

Also know where the π button and the parentheses buttons are and understand the difference between the subtraction symbol and the negative sign.

Because programmable calculators are allowed on the SAT Math test, some students may frantically program their calculator with commonly used math formulas and facts, such as: distance, the quadratic formula, midpoint, slope, circumference, area, volume, surface area, lateral surface area, the trigonometric ratios, trigonometric identities, the Pythagorean Theorem, combinations, permutations, and nth terms of geometric/arithmetic sequences. Of course, if you do not truly understand these math facts and when to use them, you end up wasting significant time scrolling through your calculator searching for them.

ON THE DAY OF THE TEST

- Make sure your calculator works! (Putting new batteries in your calculator will provide you with peace of mind.)
- Bring a backup calculator and extra batteries to the test center.

PART II
TEN PRACTICE TESTS

PRACTICE TEST 1

The following pages contain ten full-length SAT Math Level 2 Practice Tests. Treat each practice test as the actual test and complete it in one 60-minute sitting. Use the following answer sheet to fill in your multiple-choice answers. Once you have completed each practice test:

1. Check your answers using the Answer Key.
2. Review the Answers and Solutions.
3. Fill in the "Diagnose Your Strengths and Weaknesses" sheet, and determine areas that require further preparation.

PRACTICE TEST 1
MATH LEVEL 2

ANSWER SHEET

Tear out this answer sheet and use it to complete the practice test. Determine the BEST answer for each question. Then, fill in the appropriate oval using a No. 2 pencil.

1. Ⓐ Ⓑ Ⓒ Ⓓ Ⓔ	21. Ⓐ Ⓑ Ⓒ Ⓓ Ⓔ	41. Ⓐ Ⓑ Ⓒ Ⓓ Ⓔ
2. Ⓐ Ⓑ Ⓒ Ⓓ Ⓔ	22. Ⓐ Ⓑ Ⓒ Ⓓ Ⓔ	42. Ⓐ Ⓑ Ⓒ Ⓓ Ⓔ
3. Ⓐ Ⓑ Ⓒ Ⓓ Ⓔ	23. Ⓐ Ⓑ Ⓒ Ⓓ Ⓔ	43. Ⓐ Ⓑ Ⓒ Ⓓ Ⓔ
4. Ⓐ Ⓑ Ⓒ Ⓓ Ⓔ	24. Ⓐ Ⓑ Ⓒ Ⓓ Ⓔ	44. Ⓐ Ⓑ Ⓒ Ⓓ Ⓔ
5. Ⓐ Ⓑ Ⓒ Ⓓ Ⓔ	25. Ⓐ Ⓑ Ⓒ Ⓓ Ⓔ	45. Ⓐ Ⓑ Ⓒ Ⓓ Ⓔ
6. Ⓐ Ⓑ Ⓒ Ⓓ Ⓔ	26. Ⓐ Ⓑ Ⓒ Ⓓ Ⓔ	46. Ⓐ Ⓑ Ⓒ Ⓓ Ⓔ
7. Ⓐ Ⓑ Ⓒ Ⓓ Ⓔ	27. Ⓐ Ⓑ Ⓒ Ⓓ Ⓔ	47. Ⓐ Ⓑ Ⓒ Ⓓ Ⓔ
8. Ⓐ Ⓑ Ⓒ Ⓓ Ⓔ	28. Ⓐ Ⓑ Ⓒ Ⓓ Ⓔ	48. Ⓐ Ⓑ Ⓒ Ⓓ Ⓔ
9. Ⓐ Ⓑ Ⓒ Ⓓ Ⓔ	29. Ⓐ Ⓑ Ⓒ Ⓓ Ⓔ	49. Ⓐ Ⓑ Ⓒ Ⓓ Ⓔ
10. Ⓐ Ⓑ Ⓒ Ⓓ Ⓔ	30. Ⓐ Ⓑ Ⓒ Ⓓ Ⓔ	50. Ⓐ Ⓑ Ⓒ Ⓓ Ⓔ
11. Ⓐ Ⓑ Ⓒ Ⓓ Ⓔ	31. Ⓐ Ⓑ Ⓒ Ⓓ Ⓔ	
12. Ⓐ Ⓑ Ⓒ Ⓓ Ⓔ	32. Ⓐ Ⓑ Ⓒ Ⓓ Ⓔ	
13. Ⓐ Ⓑ Ⓒ Ⓓ Ⓔ	33. Ⓐ Ⓑ Ⓒ Ⓓ Ⓔ	
14. Ⓐ Ⓑ Ⓒ Ⓓ Ⓔ	34. Ⓐ Ⓑ Ⓒ Ⓓ Ⓔ	
15. Ⓐ Ⓑ Ⓒ Ⓓ Ⓔ	35. Ⓐ Ⓑ Ⓒ Ⓓ Ⓔ	
16. Ⓐ Ⓑ Ⓒ Ⓓ Ⓔ	36. Ⓐ Ⓑ Ⓒ Ⓓ Ⓔ	
17. Ⓐ Ⓑ Ⓒ Ⓓ Ⓔ	37. Ⓐ Ⓑ Ⓒ Ⓓ Ⓔ	
18. Ⓐ Ⓑ Ⓒ Ⓓ Ⓔ	38. Ⓐ Ⓑ Ⓒ Ⓓ Ⓔ	
19. Ⓐ Ⓑ Ⓒ Ⓓ Ⓔ	39. Ⓐ Ⓑ Ⓒ Ⓓ Ⓔ	
20. Ⓐ Ⓑ Ⓒ Ⓓ Ⓔ	40. Ⓐ Ⓑ Ⓒ Ⓓ Ⓔ	

PRACTICE TEST 1

Time: 60 minutes

Directions: Select the BEST answer for each of the 50 multiple-choice questions. If the exact solution is not one of the five choices, select the answer that is the best approximation. Then, fill in the appropriate oval on the answer sheet.

Notes:

1. A calculator will be needed to answer some of the questions on the test. Scientific, programmable, and graphing calculators are permitted. It is up to you to determine when and when not to use your calculator.
2. Angles on the Level 2 test are measured in degrees and radians. You need to decide whether your calculator should be set to degree mode or radian mode for a particular question.
3. Figures are drawn as accurately as possible and are intended to help solve some of the test problems. If a figure is not drawn to scale, this will be stated in the problem. All figures lie in a plane unless the problem indicates otherwise.
4. Unless otherwise stated, the domain of a function f is assumed to be the set of real numbers x for which the value of the function, $f(x)$, is a real number.
5. Reference information that may be useful in answering some of the test questions can be found below.

Reference Information	
Right circular cone with radius r and height h:	Volume $= \dfrac{1}{3}\pi r^2 h$
Right circular cone with circumference of base c and slant height ℓ:	Lateral Area $= \dfrac{1}{2}c\ell$
Sphere with radius r:	Volume $= \dfrac{4}{3}\pi r^3$ Surface Area $= 4\pi r^2$
Pyramid with base area B and height h:	Volume $= \dfrac{1}{3}Bh$

PRACTICE TEST 1 QUESTIONS

USE THIS SPACE AS SCRATCH PAPER

1. If $f(x) = 2x + 3$, the inverse of f, f^{-1}, could be represented by

   (A) $f^{-1}(x) = \dfrac{x - 3}{2}$

   (B) $f^{-1}(x) = 2x + 3$

   (C) $f^{-1}(x) = \dfrac{1}{2x + 3}$

   (D) $f^{-1}(x) = \dfrac{x + 3}{2}$

   (E) $f^{-1}(x) = \dfrac{x + 1}{2}$

2. $\tan^{-1}(\tan 124°) =$

   (A) $-124°$
   (B) $-56°$
   (C) $0°$
   (D) $56°$
   (E) $124°$

3. $x^{n+1} \cdot x^n \cdot (x^{1-n})^2 =$

   (A) x^{2n+1}
   (B) x^{n+3}
   (C) x^{n-2}
   (D) x^2
   (E) x^3

4. What is the distance between the points $(-2, -1, -3)$ and $(2, 4, 3)$?

   (A) 3.0
   (B) 5.0
   (C) 6.4
   (D) 8.8
   (E) 9.3

5. If $f(x) = 2x^2 - x + 4$, $f(-4) =$

   (A) 0
   (B) 8
   (C) 12
   (D) 32
   (E) 40

6. How many 3-student groups can be selected from a class of 30 students?

   (A) 900
   (B) 1240
   (C) 1310
   (D) 4060
   (E) 29601

GO ON TO THE NEXT PAGE

7. What is the distance of $4 - 6i$ from the origin?

    (A) 7.2
    (B) 10
    (C) 16.1
    (D) 18.8
    (E) 24

USE THIS SPACE AS SCRATCH PAPER

8. If $f(x) = 4x - 1$ and $g(x) = x^2 - 2$, then $(f + g)x =$

    (A) $5x^2 - 3$
    (B) $x^2 + 4x - 3$
    (C) $x^2 - 4x - 1$
    (D) $3x + 1$
    (E) $x - 1$

9. A player rolls the number cube and spins the spinner. What is the probability that the player will roll an odd number and spin the white section on the spinner?

    (A) $\dfrac{4}{11}$

    (B) $\dfrac{1}{2}$

    (C) $\dfrac{1}{10}$

    (D) $\dfrac{3}{4}$

    (E) $\dfrac{7}{10}$

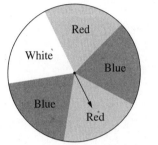

10. What is $\dfrac{2x^2 - 4x - 6}{x^2 - 9}$?

    (A) $\dfrac{2(x+1)}{x+3}$

    (B) $\dfrac{x-3}{x+3}$

    (C) $\dfrac{x+2}{x-1}$

    (D) $\dfrac{x+3}{x+1}$

    (E) $3x^2 - 4x - 15$

11. If $\sin x = -0.1324$, what is $\csc x$?

    (A) -0.132
    (B) -1.43
    (C) -1.99
    (D) -3.45
    (E) -7.55

GO ON TO THE NEXT PAGE

12. What is the value of i^{17}?

    (A) i
    (B) 1
    (C) −1
    (D) −i
    (E) 0

13. If $f(x) = ax^2 + bx + c$ and $f(1) = 0$ and $f(-1) = 2$, then $a + c$ equals

    (A) −2
    (B) 1
    (C) 0
    (D) 2
    (E) 3

14. What is the volume of the space between the sphere and cube?

    (A) 512
    (B) 368
    (C) 244
    (D) 191
    (E) 104

15. What is the area of $\triangle ABC$?

    (A) 600 cm^2
    (B) 1080 cm^2
    (C) 1350 cm^2
    (D) 2100 cm^2
    (E) 2700 cm^2

16. If point (a, b) lies on the graph of a function f, which of the following points must lie on the graph of the inverse of f?

    (A) (a, b)
    (B) $(-a, -b)$
    (C) $(-a, b)$
    (D) (b, a)
    (E) $(-b, -a)$

17. What is the product $(3 + 4i)(2 - i)$?

    (A) $2i^2 + 8i - 1$
    (B) $5i - 4$
    (C) $6i - 4$
    (D) $10i - 5$
    (E) $5i + 10$

USE THIS SPACE AS SCRATCH PAPER

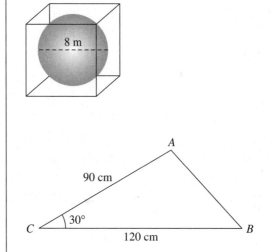

GO ON TO THE NEXT PAGE

18. According to the figure, c equals

   (A) 1

   (B) $\dfrac{b}{a}$

   (C) ab

   (D) $\dfrac{a}{b}$

   (E) -1

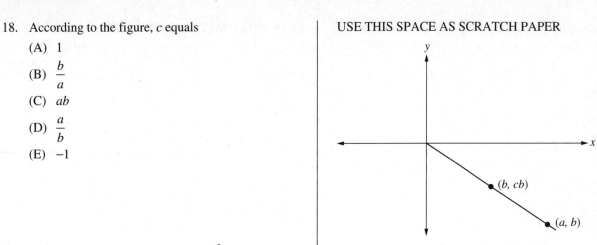

19. If $f(x) = x - 2$, $g(x) = 4x$, and $h(x) = \dfrac{3}{x}$, then $f^{-1}(g(h(3))) =$

   (A) $\dfrac{1}{4}$

   (B) 4

   (C) 6

   (D) 12

   (E) 18

20. There are 8 boys and 10 girls in the video production club. If three students are selected at random from the club, what is the probability that all of the selected students will be girls?

   (A) $\dfrac{5}{9}$

   (B) $\dfrac{5}{34}$

   (C) $\dfrac{1}{2}$

   (D) $\dfrac{10}{17}$

   (E) $\dfrac{9}{16}$

21. In a particular high school, 40 percent of the students are boys and 35 percent of the boys at this high school play an instrument. If a student at this high school were selected at random, what is the probability that the student is a boy who plays an instrument?

   (A) 0.14

   (B) 0.45

   (C) 0.60

   (D) 0.75

   (E) 0.88

GO ON TO THE NEXT PAGE

22. The slope of a line through points $A(0, -2)$ and $B(2, 6)$ is

    (A) -2

    (B) $-\dfrac{1}{2}$

    (C) 1

    (D) 4

    (E) 8

23. What is the length of side x if $\sin\theta = 0.6$?

    (A) 6 cm
    (B) 12 cm
    (C) 14 cm
    (D) 16 cm
    (E) 20 cm

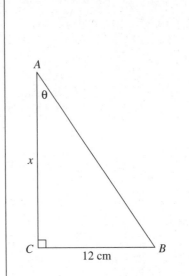

24. The slope of line $5x + 10y + 1 = 0$ is

    (A) -5

    (B) $-\dfrac{1}{2}$

    (C) $\dfrac{1}{10}$

    (D) 2

    (E) 5

25. The slope of the line perpendicular to line $2y - x + 2 = 0$ is

    (A) -2

    (B) $-\dfrac{1}{2}$

    (C) $\dfrac{1}{2}$

    (D) 2

    (E) 4

26. The polar coordinates of point P are $(0.2, 53°)$. What are the rectangular coordinates of point P?

    (A) $(0.5, 0.7)$
    (B) $(0.2, 0.12)$
    (C) $(1.2, 1.6)$
    (D) $(2.0, 1.2)$
    (E) $(0.12, 0.16)$

GO ON TO THE NEXT PAGE

27. If $f(x) = \sqrt[3]{x}$ and $g(x) = x^4 + 4$, find $(f \circ g)(2)$.

    (A) 1.3
    (B) 2.7
    (C) 15.6
    (D) 25.2
    (E) 31.7

28. The y-intercept of the line through two points whose coordinates are $(-2, 3)$ and $(6, 7)$ is

    (A) -1
    (B) $-\dfrac{1}{2}$
    (C) $\dfrac{1}{4}$
    (D) $\dfrac{1}{2}$
    (E) 4

29. What is the radian measure of $240°$?

    (A) $3\pi^R$
    (B) $\dfrac{4\pi^R}{3}$
    (C) $\dfrac{\pi^R}{4}$
    (D) $\dfrac{\pi^R}{6}$
    (E) $6\pi^R$

30. The coordinates of the vertex of the parabola whose equation is $y = 3x^2 + 12x - 12$ are

    (A) $(3, -12)$
    (B) $(-1, -6)$
    (C) $(-2, -24)$
    (D) $(9, -12)$
    (E) $(12, -12)$

31. What is the length of the longest segment whose endpoints are vertices of the rectangular solid shown?

    (A) 8.0 cm
    (B) 8.2 cm
    (C) 8.6 cm
    (D) 9.4 cm
    (E) 10.3 cm

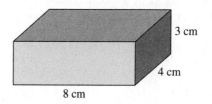

3 cm

4 cm

8 cm

GO ON TO THE NEXT PAGE

32. If $A = \begin{pmatrix} 1 & 4 \\ -3 & 2 \end{pmatrix}$ and $B = \begin{pmatrix} 0 & -1 \\ 5 & 3 \end{pmatrix}$, what is AB?

(A) $\begin{pmatrix} 20 & 11 \\ 10 & 9 \end{pmatrix}$

(B) $\begin{pmatrix} 0 & -4 \\ -15 & 6 \end{pmatrix}$

(C) $\begin{pmatrix} 10 & -41 \\ -35 & 23 \end{pmatrix}$

(D) $\begin{pmatrix} 0 & -1 \\ -15 & -9 \end{pmatrix}$

(E) $\begin{pmatrix} 0 & 3 \\ 20 & 6 \end{pmatrix}$

33. Find the zeros of $y = 2x^2 + 3x - 2$.

(A) $2, 3$

(B) $-2, \dfrac{1}{2}$

(C) $-\dfrac{3}{2}, \dfrac{1}{2}$

(D) $-1, 2$

(E) $-\dfrac{1}{2}, 1$

34. The equation of the axis of symmetry of the function $y = x^2 - 2x - 3$ is

(A) $x = 1$

(B) $x = -1$

(C) $x = \dfrac{2}{3}$

(D) $x = -\dfrac{1}{2}$

(E) $x = -\dfrac{1}{3}$

35. A student can choose any three books from a reading list of 15 books. How many different combinations of three books can the student choose?

(A) 45

(B) 90

(C) 398

(D) 455

(E) 540

36. What is the approximate area of a sector with a central angle of 5.8 radians and a circumference of 12 inches?

(A) 9

(B) 11

(C) 12

(D) 15

(E) 24

GO ON TO THE NEXT PAGE

37. Which of the following is an odd function?

    I. $2x^3 + x + 2$
    II. $6x^4 + 3x^3 - 2x^2$
    III. $5x^5 - 4x^3 + 3x$

(A) only I
(B) only II
(C) only III
(D) only I and II
(E) only II and III

38. Which of the following is a solution to $4x^2 - 2x < 2$?

(A) $-2 < x < \dfrac{1}{2}$

(B) $-\dfrac{1}{2} < x < 1$

(C) $-1 < x < 1$

(D) $\dfrac{1}{2} < x < 2$

(E) $1 < x < \dfrac{1}{4}$

39. What is the equation for the line shown?

(A) The line is undefined.
(B) $y = x - 3$
(C) $y = -3$
(D) $x = -3y$
(E) $x = -3$

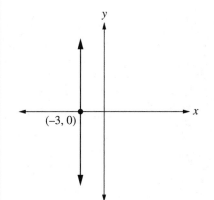

40. How many integers satisfy the inequality $x^2 - 6x < -8$?

(A) 0
(B) 1
(C) 2
(D) 4
(E) an infinite number

41. $\log_4 8 =$

(A) 0.7
(B) 1.1
(C) 1.5
(D) 1.8
(E) 2.0

GO ON TO THE NEXT PAGE

42. What is the period of $y = \dfrac{1}{2}\sin\left(\dfrac{\pi x}{3}\right)$?

    (A) $\dfrac{2}{3}$

    (B) $\dfrac{\pi}{2}$

    (C) 3π

    (D) 6

    (E) 9

43. $\sqrt[3]{4}\sqrt[9]{6}\sqrt[5]{4} =$

    (A) 1.8
    (B) 2.2
    (C) 2.4
    (D) 2.6
    (E) 2.9

44. Which of the following functions transforms $y = f(x)$ by moving it 3 units to the left?

    (A) $y = f(x+3)$
    (B) $y = f(x)+3$
    (C) $y = 3f(x)$
    (D) $y = f(x-3)$
    (E) $y = f(x)-3$

45. If $f(x) = a\begin{cases} 2x+1 & \text{when } x \neq 0 \\ 0 & \text{when } x = 0 \end{cases}$, what is the $\lim\limits_{x \to 0} f(x)$?

    (A) 0
    (B) 1
    (C) 2
    (D) 3
    (E) ∞

46. What is the determinant of $\begin{pmatrix} 3 & x \\ -1 & 4 \end{pmatrix}$?

    (A) $3x-4$
    (B) $4x-1$
    (C) $3x+4$
    (D) $12+x$
    (E) $12-x$

47. If $\cos 54° = \tan x°$, then $x =$

    (A) 1.37
    (B) 18.5
    (C) 30.4
    (D) 58.8
    (E) 88.9

GO ON TO THE NEXT PAGE

48. What is the difference between the smaller root and the larger root of the equation $2x^2 + 2x - 4 = 0$?

    (A) −1
    (B) 0
    (C) 3
    (D) 4
    (E) 6

49. The rectangular coordinates of point P are shown above. The polar coordinates of P are

    (A) $(4, 60°)$
    (B) $(5, 53°)$
    (C) $(5, 16°)$
    (D) $(4, 25°)$
    (E) $(3, 37°)$

50. Four workers can build a 40-feet tower in 4 days. At the same rate, how long would it take 8 workers to build a 60-foot tower?

    (A) 1 day
    (B) 2 days
    (C) 3 days
    (D) 4 days
    (E) 5 days

S T O P

IF YOU FINISH BEFORE TIME IS CALLED, YOU MAY CHECK YOUR WORK ON THIS TEST ONLY.
DO NOT TURN TO ANY OTHER TEST IN THIS BOOK.

ANSWER KEY

1. A	11. E	21. A	31. D	41. C
2. B	12. A	22. D	32. A	42. D
3. E	13. B	23. D	33. B	43. D
4. D	14. C	24. B	34. A	44. A
5. E	15. E	25. A	35. D	45. B
6. D	16. D	26. E	36. B	46. D
7. A	17. E	27. B	37. C	47. C
8. B	18. B	28. E	38. B	48. C
9. C	19. C	29. B	39. E	49. B
10. A	20. B	30. C	40. B	50. C

ANSWERS AND EXPLANATIONS

1. **(A)** If $y = 2x + 3$, the inverse is $x = 2y + 3$, which is equivalent to $\dfrac{x - 3}{2}$.

2. **(B)** Place your calculator in degree mode. Then enter 2nd tan^{-1} (tan 124).

3. **(E)** $x^{n+1} \cdot x^{n} \cdot (x^{1-n})^{2} = x^{n+1} \cdot x^{n} \cdot x^{2-2n} = x^{n+1+n+2-2n} = x^{3}$

4. **(D)** $d = \sqrt{(-2-2)^{2} + (-1-4)^{2} + (-3-3)^{2}} \approx 8.8$

5. **(E)** $2(-4)^{2} - (-4) + 4 = 32 + 4 + 4 = 40$

6. **(D)** Find the number of ways three items can be chosen from 30, or $C\begin{pmatrix} 30 \\ 3 \end{pmatrix} = \dfrac{30!}{3!(30-3)!} = 4060$.

7. **(A)** The distance from the origin to a complex number in the complex plane is its magnitude. It can be found according to the Pythagorean Theorem. The magnitude is $\sqrt{4^{2} + (-6^{2})} \approx 7.2$.

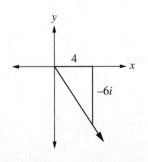

8. **(B)** $(f + g)x = f(x) + g(x); 4x - 1 + x^{2} - 2 = x^{2} + 4x - 3$

9. **(C)** $P(\text{odd, white}) = P(\text{odd}) \cdot P(\text{white}) = \dfrac{3}{6} \cdot \dfrac{1}{5} = \dfrac{3}{30} = \dfrac{1}{10}$.

10. **(A)** Factor and then cancel like terms.
$$\dfrac{2x^{2} - 4x - 6}{x^{2} - 9} = \dfrac{2(x^{2} - 2x - 3)}{(x+3)(x-3)} = \dfrac{2(x-3)(x+1)}{(x+3)(x-3)}$$
$$= \dfrac{2(x+1)}{3}.$$

11. **(E)** $\csc x = \dfrac{1}{\sin x} = \dfrac{1}{-0.1324} = -7.55$.

12. **(A)** $i^{17} = i^{16+1} = (i^{4})^{4} \cdot i = 1 \cdot i = i$

13. **(B)** Substitute 0 for x to get $a + b + c = 0$. Substitute -1 for x to get $a - b + c = 2$. Add these two equations to get $2a + 2c = 2$, and then $a + c = 1$.

14. **(C)** The volume of the sphere is $\dfrac{4}{3}\pi(4)^{3} \approx 268$ m^{3}.

The side length of the cube is the diameter of the sphere, 8 m, so the volume of the cube is 512 m^{3}. The volume of the space is the difference between the volume of the cube and the volume of the sphere, 512 m^{3} – 268 m^{3} = 244 m^{3}.

15. **(E)** Area $= \frac{1}{2}ab \sin C = \frac{1}{2} \cdot 120 \cdot 90 \cdot \sin 30° = \frac{1}{2} \cdot 120 \cdot 90 \cdot \frac{1}{2} = 2700$ cm².

16. **(D)** Inverse functions are symmetric about the line $b = a$. Therefore, if point (a, b) lies on f, point (b, a) must lie on f^{-1}.

17. **(E)** $(3 + 4i)(2 - i) = 6 + 8i - 3i - 4i^2 = 6 + 5i - 4(-1) = 6 + 5i + 4 = 5i + 10$.

18. **(B)** First find the slope of the line through (a, b) and $(0, 0)$, which is $\frac{b}{a}$. Then find the slope of the line through (b, cb) and $(0, 0)$, which is $\frac{cb}{b} = c$. The two slopes must be equal, so $c = \frac{b}{a}$.

19. **(C)** $h(3) = 1$. $g(1) = 4$. Interchange x and y to find that $f^{-1}(x) = x + 2$, so $f^{-1}(4) = 6$.

20. **(B)** The probability that the first student selected will be a girl is $\frac{10}{18}$. For the next selection, there are only 17 students left, 9 of which are girls, so the probability that the second student is also a girl is $\frac{9}{17}$. The probability that the third student is also a girl is $\frac{8}{16}$. The overall probability that the three students are all girls is $\frac{10}{18} \cdot \frac{9}{17} \cdot \frac{8}{16} = \frac{720}{4896} = \frac{5}{34}$.

21. **(A)** The probability is $(0.40)(0.35) = 0.14$.

22. **(D)** Slope $= \frac{-2 - 6}{0 - 2} = \frac{-8}{-2} = 4$

23. **(D)** $\sin \theta = \frac{\text{opposite}}{\text{hypotenuse}}$, so $0.6 = \frac{12}{AB}$ and $AB = 20$ cm. $x = \sqrt{20^2 - 12^2} = 16$.

24. **(B)** Rewrite the equation in terms of y. $10y = -5x - 1$. $y = -\frac{5}{10x} - \frac{1}{10} = -\frac{1}{2x} - \frac{1}{10}$. The slope is $-\frac{1}{2}$.

25. **(A)** Rewrite the equation in terms of y: $y = \frac{1}{2x} - 1$. The slope of the line is $\frac{1}{2}$. The slope of a perpendicular line is the negative reciprocal, which is -2.

26. **(E)** With your calculator set to degrees, find $x = R \cos t = 0.2 \cos 53 = 0.12$ and $y = R \sin t = 0.16$.

27. **(B)** One method is to enter f in Y_1 and g in Y_2, return to the home screen and enter $Y_1(Y_2(2))$. Another method is to solve for $g(x)$, and then solve for $f(g(x))$. $g(2) = 24 + 4 = 20$. $f(g(2)) = \sqrt[3]{20} \approx 2.7$.

28. **(E)** The slope of the line is $\frac{3 - 7}{-2 - 6} = \frac{1}{2}$, so the point-slope equation is $y - 7 = \frac{1}{2}(x - 6)$. Solve for y to get $y = \frac{1}{2x} + 4$. The y-intercept of the line is 4.

29. **(B)** Multiply 240° by $\frac{\pi}{180°}$, which yields $240°\left(\frac{\pi}{180°}\right) = \frac{4\pi^R}{3}$.

30. **(C)** The x-coordinate of the vertex is $x = -\frac{b}{2a} = -\frac{12}{6} = -2$ and the y-coordinate is $y = 3(-2)^2 + 12(-2) - 12 = -24$. Therefore, the vertex is the point $(-2, -24)$.

31. **(D)** The longest segment will be a diagonal of the solid. The length of the diagonal is $d = \sqrt{(3)^2 + (4)^2 + (8)^2} \approx 9.4$.

32. **(A)** $\begin{pmatrix} 1 & 4 \\ -3 & 2 \end{pmatrix}\begin{pmatrix} 0 & -1 \\ 5 & 3 \end{pmatrix} = $

$\begin{pmatrix} (1 \cdot 0) + (4 \cdot 5) & (1 \cdot -1) + (4 \cdot 3) \\ (-3 \cdot 0) + (2 \cdot 5) & (-3 \cdot -1) + (2 \cdot 3) \end{pmatrix} = \begin{pmatrix} 20 & 11 \\ 10 & 9 \end{pmatrix}$

33. **(B)** $2x^2 + 3x - 2 = (2x - 1)(x + 2) = 0$, so the zeros are $\frac{1}{2}$ and -2.

34. **(A)** The x-coordinate of the vertex is $-\frac{b}{2a} = \left(-\frac{-2}{2}\right) = 1$. The equation of the axis of symmetry is, therefore, $x = 1$.

35. **(D)** The order of the books does not matter, so the answer is the result of combination:

$$\frac{15!}{(15 - 3)!3!} = \frac{15!}{12!3!} = 455.$$

36. **(B)** $C = 2\pi r = 12$, so $r = \frac{6}{\pi} \approx 1.91$. $A = \frac{1}{2}r^2\theta = \frac{1}{2}(1.91)^2(5.8) \approx 11$.

37. **(C)** An odd function has only odd exponents and no constant term.

38. **(B)** $4x^2 - 2x - 2 = (2x + 1)(2x - 2) = 0$ when $x = -\frac{1}{2}$ or 1. Therefore, numbers between these values satisfy the inequality.

39. **(E)** The line is vertical so the slope is undefined. Therefore, there is no coefficient of the x in the slope-intercept form of a line and the line has the format $x = c$, where c is a constant. The line passes through the point $(-3, 0)$, so the equation of the line is $x = -3$.

40. **(B)** $x^2 - 6x + 8 = (x - 2)(x - 4) = 0$ when $x = 2$ or 4. Integers between these satisfy the original inequality.

41. **(C)** $\log_4 8 = \dfrac{\log 8}{\log 4} \approx \dfrac{0.903}{0.602} \approx 1.5$.

42. **(D)** Rewrite as $y = \dfrac{1}{2}\sin\left(\dfrac{\pi}{3}\right)x$. The period $= \dfrac{2\pi}{\dfrac{\pi}{3}} = 6$.

43. **(D)** $\sqrt[3]{4}\sqrt[9]{6}\sqrt[5]{4} = 4^{\frac{1}{3}}4^{\frac{1}{9}}4^{\frac{1}{5}} = 2.6$

44. **(A)** $y = f(x - h)$ translates to $y = f(x)$ h units horizontally. The translation is to the left if $h < 0$.

45. **(B)** As x approaches zero, $2x + 1$ approaches 1, even though $f(x) = 0$ when $x = 0$. Therefore, $\lim\limits_{x \to 0} f(x) = 1$.

46. **(D)** The determinant $= (3 \cdot 4) - (-1 \cdot x) = 12 - (-x) = 12 + x$.

47. **(C)** With your calculator in degree mode, evaluate $\tan^{-1}(\cos 54°)$.

48. **(C)** One method is to use your calculator to find the roots according to the quadratic formula, and then subtract the smaller root from the larger root. Another method is to substitute the values of a, b, and c into the quadratic formula to find the algebraic solutions, and then subtract to find the difference. $x = \dfrac{-2 \pm \sqrt{4 + 32}}{4} = \dfrac{-2 \pm 6}{4}$; the roots are 1 and -2, so the difference is $1 - (-2) = 3$.

49. **(B)** $r^2 = x^2 + y^2 = 9 + 16 = 25$ so $r = 5$. $r \cos\theta = x$, so $\cos\theta = \dfrac{3}{5}$. Therefore, $\theta = 53°$, so the polar coordinates are $(5, 53°)$.

50. **(C)** The 4 workers completed 10 feet of tower per day, which equates to 2.5 feet per worker per day. At the same rate, 8 workers would complete 20 feet of tower per day $(2.5 \times 8 = 20)$. They would therefore need 3 days to complete the 60-foot tower.

▮▮▮ DIAGNOSE YOUR STRENGTHS AND WEAKNESSES

Check the number of each question answered correctly and "X" the number of each question answered incorrectly.

Algebra and Functions	1	3	5	8	10	13	16	18	19	22	24	25	27	Total Number Correct
25 questions														
	28	30	33	34	37	38	40	41	43	45	48	50		

Trigonometry	2	11	15	23	29	36	42	47	Total Number Correct
8 questions									

Coordinate and Three-Dimensional Geometry	4	14	26	31	39	44	49	Total Number Correct
7 questions								

Numbers and Operations	6	7	12	17	32	46	Total Number Correct
6 questions							

Data Analysis, Statistics, and Probability	9	20	21	35	Total Number Correct
4 questions					

Number of correct answers − $\frac{1}{4}$ (Number of incorrect answers) = Your raw score

$$\underline{\hspace{6cm}} - \frac{1}{4} (\underline{\hspace{6cm}}) = \underline{\hspace{3cm}}$$

Compare your raw score with the approximate SAT Subject Test score below:

	Raw Score	SAT Subject Test Approximate Score
Excellent	43–50	770–800
Very Good	33–43	670–770
Good	27–33	620–670
Above Average	21–27	570–620
Average	11–21	500–570
Below Average	< 11	< 500

PRACTICE TEST 2

Treat this practice test as the actual test and complete it in one 60-minute sitting. Use the following answer sheet to fill in your multiple-choice answers. Once you have completed the practice test:

1. Check your answers using the Answer Key.
2. Review the Answers and Solutions.
3. Fill in the "Diagnose Your Strengths and Weaknesses" sheet, and determine areas that require further preparation.

PRACTICE TEST 2

MATH LEVEL 2

ANSWER SHEET

Tear out this answer sheet and use it to complete the practice test. Determine the BEST answer for each question. Then, fill in the appropriate oval using a No. 2 pencil.

1. (A) (B) (C) (D) (E)	21. (A) (B) (C) (D) (E)	41. (A) (B) (C) (D) (E)	
2. (A) (B) (C) (D) (E)	22. (A) (B) (C) (D) (E)	42. (A) (B) (C) (D) (E)	
3. (A) (B) (C) (D) (E)	23. (A) (B) (C) (D) (E)	43. (A) (B) (C) (D) (E)	
4. (A) (B) (C) (D) (E)	24. (A) (B) (C) (D) (E)	44. (A) (B) (C) (D) (E)	
5. (A) (B) (C) (D) (E)	25. (A) (B) (C) (D) (E)	45. (A) (B) (C) (D) (E)	
6. (A) (B) (C) (D) (E)	26. (A) (B) (C) (D) (E)	46. (A) (B) (C) (D) (E)	
7. (A) (B) (C) (D) (E)	27. (A) (B) (C) (D) (E)	47. (A) (B) (C) (D) (E)	
8. (A) (B) (C) (D) (E)	28. (A) (B) (C) (D) (E)	48. (A) (B) (C) (D) (E)	
9. (A) (B) (C) (D) (E)	29. (A) (B) (C) (D) (E)	49. (A) (B) (C) (D) (E)	
10. (A) (B) (C) (D) (E)	30. (A) (B) (C) (D) (E)	50. (A) (B) (C) (D) (E)	
11. (A) (B) (C) (D) (E)	31. (A) (B) (C) (D) (E)		
12. (A) (B) (C) (D) (E)	32. (A) (B) (C) (D) (E)		
13. (A) (B) (C) (D) (E)	33. (A) (B) (C) (D) (E)		
14. (A) (B) (C) (D) (E)	34. (A) (B) (C) (D) (E)		
15. (A) (B) (C) (D) (E)	35. (A) (B) (C) (D) (E)		
16. (A) (B) (C) (D) (E)	36. (A) (B) (C) (D) (E)		
17. (A) (B) (C) (D) (E)	37. (A) (B) (C) (D) (E)		
18. (A) (B) (C) (D) (E)	38. (A) (B) (C) (D) (E)		
19. (A) (B) (C) (D) (E)	39. (A) (B) (C) (D) (E)		
20. (A) (B) (C) (D) (E)	40. (A) (B) (C) (D) (E)		

PRACTICE TEST 2

Time: 60 minutes

Directions: Select the BEST answer for each of the 50 multiple-choice questions. If the exact solution is not one of the five choices, select the answer that is the best approximation. Then, fill in the appropriate oval on the answer sheet.

Notes:

1. A calculator will be needed to answer some of the questions on the test. Scientific, programmable, and graphing calculators are permitted. It is up to you to determine when and when not to use your calculator.
2. Angles on the Level 2 test are measured in degrees and radians. You need to decide whether your calculator should be set to degree mode or radian mode for a particular question.
3. Figures are drawn as accurately as possible and are intended to help solve some of the test problems. If a figure is not drawn to scale, this will be stated in the problem. All figures lie in a plane unless the problem indicates otherwise.
4. Unless otherwise stated, the domain of a function f is assumed to be the set of real numbers x for which the value of the function, $f(x)$, is a real number.
5. Reference information that may be useful in answering some of the test questions can be found below.

Reference Information	
Right circular cone with radius r and height h:	Volume $= \dfrac{1}{3}\pi r^2 h$
Right circular cone with circumference of base c and slant height ℓ:	Lateral Area $= \dfrac{1}{2}c\ell$
Sphere with radius r:	Volume $= \dfrac{4}{3}\pi r^3$
	Surface Area $= 4\pi r^2$
Pyramid with base area B and height h:	Volume $= \dfrac{1}{3}Bh$

PRACTICE TEST 2 QUESTIONS

1. Which of the following relations are odd?

   I $y = 5$
   II $y = x$
   III $x^2 + y^2 = 1$

   (A) only I
   (B) only I and II
   (C) only I and III
   (D) only II and III
   (E) I, II, and III

2. Find the matrix equation that represents the system
   $$\begin{cases} 4x - 2 = y \\ y + 3x = 12 \end{cases}$$

   (A) $\begin{pmatrix} 4 & x \\ 1 & y \end{pmatrix}\begin{pmatrix} 2 \\ x \end{pmatrix} = \begin{pmatrix} y \\ 12 \end{pmatrix}$

   (B) $\begin{pmatrix} 4 & 1 \\ 3 & 1 \end{pmatrix}\begin{pmatrix} x \\ y \end{pmatrix} = \begin{pmatrix} 2 \\ 12 \end{pmatrix}$

   (C) $\begin{pmatrix} 2 \\ 12 \end{pmatrix}(x \quad y) = \begin{pmatrix} 4 & -1 \\ 1 & 3 \end{pmatrix}$

   (D) $\begin{pmatrix} 4 & -2 \\ 1 & 3 \end{pmatrix}\begin{pmatrix} x \\ y \end{pmatrix} = \begin{pmatrix} 1 \\ 12 \end{pmatrix}$

   (E) $\begin{pmatrix} 4 & -1 \\ 3 & 1 \end{pmatrix}\begin{pmatrix} x \\ y \end{pmatrix} = \begin{pmatrix} 2 \\ 12 \end{pmatrix}$

3. The graph below shows part of the graph for $y = \sin 4x$. What are the coordinates of point R?

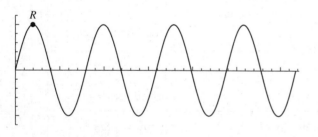

   (A) $\left(\dfrac{\pi}{8}, 1\right)$

   (B) $(\pi, 1)$

   (C) $\left(\dfrac{\pi}{4}, 2\right)$

   (D) $(2\pi, 4)$

   (E) $(\pi, 2)$

GO ON TO THE NEXT PAGE

4. What is the distance between two points in space, $E(2, -1, 1)$ and $F(1, 1, 0)$?

    (A) 1.2
    (B) 2.4
    (C) 3.1
    (D) 3.7
    (E) 5.8

5. What value(s) must be excluded from the domain of

    $$f = \left\{ (x, y) : y = \frac{x+3}{x-3} \right\}?$$

    (A) −3
    (B) 0
    (C) 3
    (D) 3 and −3
    (E) no value

6. A point on the ground is a horizontal distance of 80 feet from the bottom of a building. The angle of elevation from the point to the top of the building is 58°. What is the height of the building?

    (A) 22 ft
    (B) 57 ft
    (C) 68 ft
    (D) 92 ft
    (E) 128 ft

7. If $p(x) = 6x - 2$ and $p(a) = 1$, then $a =$

    (A) $\dfrac{1}{4}$
    (B) $\dfrac{1}{2}$
    (C) 1
    (D) 4
    (E) 12

8. An instructor found that the mean of 20 students' test scores was 88.5. One more student takes the test and raises the mean by 0.3 point. What did the student score on the test?

    (A) 88
    (B) 90
    (C) 93
    (D) 95
    (E) 98

GO ON TO THE NEXT PAGE

9. If $\log_{27} 3 = x$, what is the value of x?

    (A) $\dfrac{1}{9}$

    (B) $\dfrac{1}{6}$

    (C) $\dfrac{1}{4}$

    (D) $\dfrac{1}{3}$

    (E) $\dfrac{1}{2}$

10. What is the domain of $f(x) = \sqrt[3]{12 - x^2}$?

    (A) $x > 0$
    (B) $x > 2.29$
    (C) $-1.44 < x < 1.44$
    (D) $-2.29 < x < 2.29$
    (E) all real numbers

11. If $f(x) = x^2$, then $\dfrac{f(x+r) - f(x)}{r} =$

    (A) $2x + r$
    (B) $x^2 + 2xr + r^2$
    (C) $2xr + r^2$
    (D) $2x$
    (E) $r + 1$

12. What is the midpoint of the line segment that connects the two points shown?

    (A) $(-2, 2)$
    (B) $(-1, 1)$
    (C) $(0, 1)$
    (D) $(1, 2)$
    (E) $(2, -1)$

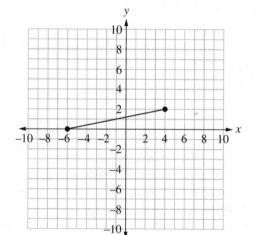

13. What value of y will make the following system of equations true?

$$2x + y = 3$$
$$4x - y = 0$$

    (A) $\dfrac{1}{2}$

    (B) 1
    (C) 2

    (D) $\dfrac{3}{4}$

    (E) 4

GO ON TO THE NEXT PAGE

14. If $f(x) = x - \dfrac{1}{x}$, then $f(x) + f\left(\dfrac{1}{x}\right) =$

    (A) x

    (B) $\dfrac{1}{x}$

    (C) 0

    (D) 1

    (E) $2x$

15. If $f(x) = x^2 - bx$, then $f(b) =$

    (A) b

    (B) 0

    (C) $b - 1$

    (D) b^2

    (E) 1

16. What is $\cos 120°$ in terms of θ_r?

    (A) $-\cos 60°$

    (B) $-\cos 20°$

    (C) $\cos 20°$

    (D) $\cos 60°$

    (E) $\cos 80°$

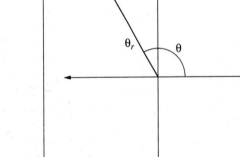

17. A linear function has an x-intercept of $\sqrt{6}$ and a y-intercept of $\sqrt{8}$. The graph of the function has a slope of

    (A) -0.87

    (B) -1.15

    (C) 1.41

    (D) 2.45

    (E) 2.83

18. There are 20 students in the math club. A team of four students will be selected at random to represent the club at a contest. How many different teams are possible?

    (A) 80

    (B) 1920

    (C) 2433

    (D) 4845

    (E) 40320

GO ON TO THE NEXT PAGE

19. Four friends—Sam, Juan, Lee, and Paul—sit in a row at a movie. What is the probability that Sam is at either end in the row?

(A) $\dfrac{1}{2}$

(B) $\dfrac{1}{3}$

(C) $\dfrac{1}{4}$

(D) $\dfrac{1}{8}$

(E) $\dfrac{1}{12}$

20. The slope of a line through points $A(-2, -2)$ and $B(4, 1)$ is

(A) $\dfrac{1}{4}$

(B) $\dfrac{1}{2}$

(C) 1

(D) $1\dfrac{1}{2}$

(E) 5

21. $\tan^{-1}(\tan 114) =$

(A) −66

(B) −2.2

(C) 2.2

(D) 66

(E) 91

22. The slope of line $3x + 6y + 4 = 0$ is

(A) $-\dfrac{4}{3}$

(B) $-\dfrac{1}{2}$

(C) $\dfrac{3}{4}$

(D) 3

(E) 6

23. By what factor does volume increase if the height and radius of a cylinder are both doubled?

(A) 2

(B) 3

(C) 4

(D) 8

(E) 16

USE THIS SPACE AS SCRATCH PAPER

GO ON TO THE NEXT PAGE

24. The slope of the line perpendicular to line $3y - 2x - 12 = 0$ is

   (A) $-\dfrac{3}{2}$

   (B) -1

   (C) $\dfrac{2}{3}$

   (D) 2

   (E) 3

25. The y-intercept of the line through two points whose coordinates are $(-2, 8)$ and $(3, -2)$ is

   (A) -4

   (B) -2

   (C) 4

   (D) 6

   (E) 10

26. The coordinates of the vertex of the parabola whose equation is $y = 3x^2 + 6x - 1$ are

   (A) $(3, 6)$

   (B) $(-1, -4)$

   (C) $(-1, 8)$

   (D) $(9, -1)$

   (E) $(1, -3)$

27. If $A = (-2 \ \ 1 \ \ 3)$ and $B = \begin{pmatrix} 0 & 5 & -2 \\ 1 & -3 & 0 \\ 4 & 6 & -4 \end{pmatrix}$, what is AB?

   (A) $(13 \ \ 5 \ \ -8)$

   (B) $\begin{pmatrix} 13 \\ -4 \\ 18 \end{pmatrix}$

   (C) $\begin{pmatrix} 0 \\ -3 \\ 12 \end{pmatrix}$

   (D) $\begin{pmatrix} 0 & 5 & -6 \\ -2 & -3 & 0 \\ -8 & 6 & -12 \end{pmatrix}$

   (E) $\begin{pmatrix} 0 & -10 & 4 \\ 1 & -3 & 0 \\ 12 & 18 & -12 \end{pmatrix}$

28. The range of the function $f = \{(x, y): y = 8 - 6x - x^2\}$ is

   (A) $\{y: y \leq 1\}$

   (B) $\{y: y \geq 0\}$

   (C) $\{y: y \geq 17\}$

   (D) $\{y: y \leq 9\}$

   (E) $\{y: y \leq 17\}$

USE THIS SPACE AS SCRATCH PAPER

GO ON TO THE NEXT PAGE

29. Which is the period of $y = \frac{1}{2} \cos\left(\frac{2x}{3}\right)$?

    (A) 2π
    (B) 3π
    (C) $\frac{2\pi}{3}$
    (D) $\frac{1}{2\pi}$
    (E) $\frac{\pi}{2}$

30. Find the zeros of $y = x^2 - x - 6$.

    (A) $2, 3$
    (B) $-6, 1$
    (C) $-3, 0$
    (D) $-2, 3$
    (E) $-1, 6$

31. The equation of the axis of symmetry of the function $y = 2x^2 + 4x - 6$ is

    (A) $x = 1$
    (B) $x = -1$
    (C) $x = 2$
    (D) $x = -\frac{1}{2}$
    (E) $x = -\frac{1}{3}$

32. What is the length of a in the triangle below?

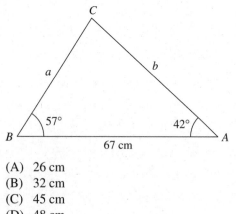

    (A) 26 cm
    (B) 32 cm
    (C) 45 cm
    (D) 48 cm
    (E) 57 cm

33. If the repeating decimal $0.\overline{55}$ is written as a fraction in lowest terms, what is the sum of the numerator and denominator?

    (A) 5
    (B) 12
    (C) 14
    (D) 17
    (E) 23

GO ON TO THE NEXT PAGE

34. Which radian measure is equivalent to 20°?

(A) $9\pi^R$

(B) $\dfrac{\pi^R}{9}$

(C) 9

(D) $\dfrac{\pi^R}{6}$

(E) $\dfrac{2\pi^R}{3}$

35. What is the sum of the zeros of $y = x^2 - 5x + 6$?

(A) −4
(B) 3
(C) 5
(D) 6
(E) 10

36. Which point on the graph represents $-2 - 3i$?

(A) *A*
(B) *B*
(C) *C*
(D) *D*
(E) *E*

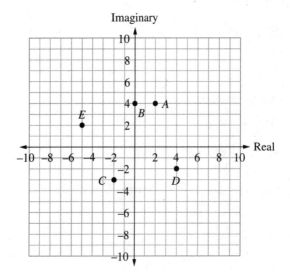

37. A student tosses a coin three times. What is the probability that exactly two tails will appear?

(A) $\dfrac{1}{4}$

(B) $\dfrac{3}{8}$

(C) $\dfrac{1}{2}$

(D) $\dfrac{2}{7}$

(E) $\dfrac{3}{4}$

GO ON TO THE NEXT PAGE

38. The volume of a cube is six times the volume of a sphere. What is the ratio of the side of the cube to the radius of the sphere?

    (A) $\sqrt{2\pi}$

    (B) $\sqrt[3]{8\pi}$

    (C) $\sqrt[3]{4\pi}$

    (D) $\sqrt[6]{4\pi}$

    (E) $\sqrt[6]{8\pi}$

39. What is the distance between the points with coordinates $(-2, 3, 5)$ and $(4, -2, 1)$?

    (A) 2.4
    (B) 3.8
    (C) 6.2
    (D) 8.8
    (E) 10.1

40. Which function below could be represented by the graph?

    (A) $y = 2 \sin x$

    (B) $y = \dfrac{1}{2} \sin 2x$

    (C) $y = 2 \sin 2x$
    (D) $y = \sin x$

    (E) $y = \dfrac{1}{2} \sin \dfrac{x}{2}$

USE THIS SPACE AS SCRATCH PAPER

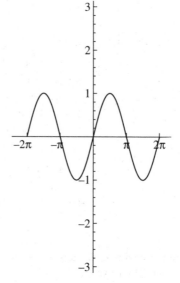

GO ON TO THE NEXT PAGE

41. Which of the following lines is perpendicular to the one shown?

    (A) $2x + y = -1$
    (B) $x - y = 3$
    (C) $y = \dfrac{1}{2}x + 3$
    (D) $2y = x + 6$
    (E) $\dfrac{1}{2}y - x = +2$

USE THIS SPACE AS SCRATCH PAPER

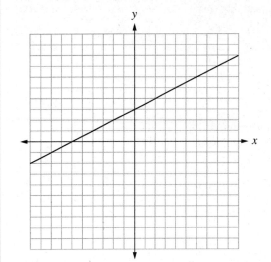

42. Which point describes the center of circle $x^2 + y^2 - 4x + 10y = -20$?

    (A) $(-4, 10)$
    (B) $(2, -5)$
    (C) $(5, 2)$
    (D) $(1, -4)$
    (E) $(0, 0)$

43. What is the modulus of $4 + 3i$?

    (A) $\sqrt{5}$
    (B) 5
    (C) 2
    (D) $\sqrt{7}$
    (E) $2\sqrt{3}$

44. $\dfrac{10\sqrt{96}}{2\sqrt{2}} =$

    (A) $20\sqrt{3}$
    (B) $5\sqrt{2}$
    (C) $10\sqrt{4}$
    (D) $2\sqrt{6}$
    (E) $12\sqrt{3}$

GO ON TO THE NEXT PAGE

45. If $4x^3 - 8x^2 + Mx - 14$ is divisible by $x - 2$, what is the value of M?

   (A) −4
   (B) −2
   (C) 2
   (D) 7
   (E) 14

46. What are the coordinates of the vertex of the parabola whose equation is $y = (x - 3)^2 + 4$?

   (A) $(4, 3)$
   (B) $(-3, 4)$
   (C) $(3, 4)$
   (D) $(3, -4)$
   (E) $(4, -3)$

47. Angle θ is in standard position with its terminal side in the third quadrant. What is the exact value of $\cos \theta$ if $\sin \theta = \dfrac{1}{2}$?

   (A) $\dfrac{\sqrt{3}}{2}$

   (B) $\sqrt{3}$

   (C) $\dfrac{1}{2}$

   (D) $-\dfrac{\sqrt{3}}{2}$

   (E) $-\sqrt{3}$

48. What is the range of the data 23, 48, 28, 30, 23, 32?

   (A) 23
   (B) 25
   (C) 28
   (D) 31
   (E) 48

49. What is the product of $(2 + 3i)(2 - 3i)$?

   (A) 7
   (B) $5i$
   (C) $9i$
   (D) 13
   (E) $13 - i$

GO ON TO THE NEXT PAGE

50. Which equation describes the line represented below?

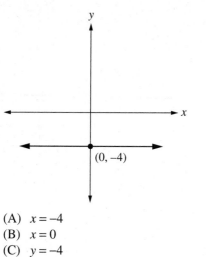

(A) $x = -4$
(B) $x = 0$
(C) $y = -4$
(D) $y = 0$
(E) This line is undefined.

S T O P

IF YOU FINISH BEFORE TIME IS CALLED, YOU MAY CHECK YOUR WORK ON THIS TEST ONLY.
DO NOT TURN TO ANY OTHER TEST IN THIS BOOK.

ANSWER KEY

1. D	11. A	21. A	31. B	41. A
2. E	12. B	22. B	32. C	42. B
3. A	13. C	23. D	33. C	43. B
4. B	14. C	24. A	34. B	44. A
5. C	15. B	25. C	35. C	45. D
6. E	16. A	26. B	36. C	46. C
7. B	17. B	27. A	37. B	47. D
8. D	18. D	28. E	38. B	48. B
9. D	19. A	29. B	39. D	49. D
10. E	20. B	30. D	40. D	50. C

ANSWERS AND EXPLANATIONS

1. **(D)** Analyze each relation.

   I. The graph of $y = 5$ is a horizontal line, which is not symmetric about the origin. This relation is not odd.

   II. Since $f(-x) = -x = -f(x)$, this function is odd.

   III. Since $(-x)^2 + (-y)^2 = 1$ whenever $x^2 + y^2 = 1$, this relation is odd.

2. **(E)** Write the system in standard form $\begin{cases} 4x - y = 2 \\ 3x + y = 12 \end{cases}$. Use the coefficients $\begin{pmatrix} 4 & -1 \\ 3 & 1 \end{pmatrix}$, variables $\begin{pmatrix} x \\ y \end{pmatrix}$, and constants $\begin{pmatrix} 2 \\ 12 \end{pmatrix}$ to find the matrix equation.

3. **(A)** The period of the wave is $\frac{\pi}{2}$. The point is located $\frac{1}{4}$ way through the period, so the x-coordinate is $\frac{\pi}{8}$. The amplitude is 1 because the coefficient of sin is 1.

4. **(B)** $d = \sqrt{(2-1)^2 + (-1-1)^2 + (1-0)^2} = 2.4$

5. **(C)** Division by 0 is not possible. Therefore, x cannot equal 3.

6. **(E)** Draw a diagram to represent the situation.

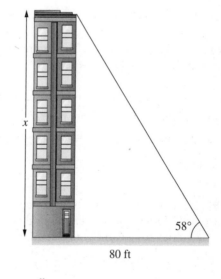

$\tan 58° = \dfrac{x}{80}$, $x = 80 \tan 58° = 128$.

7. **(B)** $p(a) = 1$ implies that $6a - 2 = 1$, so $a = \dfrac{1}{2}$.

8. **(D)** The total of the first 20 students' scores is $20 \cdot 88.5 = 1770$. The total of 21 scores is $21 \cdot 88.8 = 1865$. The difference, $1865 - 1770$, is 95.

9. **(D)** $27^x = 3$, so $(3^3)^x = 3$, which means that $3^{3x} = 3$. Therefore, $3x = 1$ and $x = \dfrac{1}{3}$.

10. **(E)** The domain of the cube root function is all real numbers. Therefore, x can be any real number.

11. **(A)** $f(x + r) = (x + r)^2 = x^2 + 2xr + r^2$. So $f(x + r) - f(x) = x^2 + 2xr + r^2 - x^2$. Divide this expression by r to get the correct answer choice.

12. **(B)** midpoint $= \left(\dfrac{-6+4}{2}, \dfrac{0+2}{2} \right) = \left(\dfrac{-2}{2}, \dfrac{2}{2} \right) = (-1, 1)$.

13. **(C)** Rearrange the first equation as $y = 3 - 2x$. Substitute this value of y into the second equation: $4x - (3 - 2x) = 0$. Solve to find that $x = \dfrac{1}{2}$. Substitute this value of x in the first original equation: $2\left(\dfrac{1}{2}\right) + y = 3$. Solve to find that $y = 2$. Another method is to multiply the top equation by -2 to get $-4x - 2y = 3$. Add the new equation to the second equation to eliminate the x term and get $-3y = -6$, so $y = 2$.

14. **(C)** $f(x) = x - \dfrac{1}{x}$ and $f\left(\dfrac{1}{x}\right) = f(x) = \dfrac{1}{x} - x$. Therefore, $f(x) + f\left(\dfrac{1}{x}\right) = 0$.

15. **(B)** Replace x with b. $f(b) = b^2 - b(b) = b^2 - b^2 = 0$.

16. **(A)** $\theta_r = 180° - 120° = 60°$. The cosine is negative in quadrant II, so $\cos 120° = -\cos 60°$.

17. **(B)** $y = mx + b$. You can use the x-intercept to find $0 = m\sqrt{6} + b$, and the y-intercept to find $\sqrt{8} = m \cdot 0 + b$. Therefore, $0 = m\sqrt{6} + \sqrt{8}$ and $m = -\dfrac{\sqrt{8}}{\sqrt{6}} \approx -1.15$.

18. **(D)** The problem involves a combination because order does not matter. To find the answer, enter the values for $_{20}C_4$ in your calculator to solve. Or find the solution as $C(4, 20) = \dfrac{20!}{4!(20-4)!}$.

19. **(A)** There are four positions in the row. The ends make up two of those positions, or $\dfrac{1}{2}$. Therefore, $P(\text{Sam in an end seat}) = \dfrac{1}{2}$.

20. **(B)** Slope $= \dfrac{-2-1}{-2-4} = \dfrac{-3}{-6} = \dfrac{1}{2}$.

21. **(A)** With your calculator set to degree mode, enter 2nd $\tan^{-1}(\tan 114)$ to find the answer.

22. **(B)** Rewrite the equation in terms of y. $6y = -3x - 4$. $y = -\dfrac{3}{6}x - \dfrac{4}{3} = -\dfrac{1}{2}x - \dfrac{4}{3}$. The slope is $-\dfrac{1}{2}$. Another method is to rewrite the equation as $Ax + By = C$, where $m = -\left(\dfrac{A}{B}\right)$. $3x + 6y = -4$, therefore $m = -\left(\dfrac{3}{6}\right)$ or $-\dfrac{1}{2}$.

23. **(D)** $V = \pi r^2 h$, $V = \pi (2r)^2 2h$, $V = \pi 4r^2 2h$, $V = 8(\pi r^2 h)$.

24. **(A)** Rewrite the equation in terms of y. $y = \dfrac{2}{3}x + 4$. The slope of the line is $\dfrac{2}{3}$. The slope of a perpendicular line is the negative reciprocal, which is $-\dfrac{3}{2}$.

25. **(C)** The slope of the line is $\dfrac{8-(-2)}{-2-3} = -2$, so the point-slope equation is $y - (-2) = -2(x - 3)$. Solve for y to get $y = -2x + 4$. The y-intercept of the line is 4.

26. **(B)** The x coordinate of the vertex is $x = \dfrac{-b}{2a} = -\dfrac{6}{6} = -1$ and the y-coordinate is $y = 3(-1)^2 + 6(-1) - 1 = -4$. Therefore, the vertex is the point $(-1, -4)$.

27. **(A)** Multiply to find the product:

$((-2 \cdot 0) + (1 \cdot 1) + (3 \cdot 4) \quad (-2 \cdot 5) + (1 \cdot -3) + (3 \cdot 6)$
$(-2 \cdot 2) + (1 \cdot 0) + (3 \cdot -4))$.

28. **(E)** The vertex is $x = -\dfrac{b}{2a} = -\left(\dfrac{-6}{-2}\right) = -3$ and $y = 8 - 6(-3) - (-3)^2 = 17$. Because $a = -1 < 0$, the parabola opens down, so the range is $\{y : y \le 17\}$.

29. **(B)** Rewrite as $y = \dfrac{1}{2}\cos\left(\dfrac{2}{3}\right)x$. Period $= \dfrac{2\pi}{\frac{2}{3}} = 3\pi$.

30. **(D)** $x^2 - x - 6 = (x - 3)(x + 2) = 0$, so the zeros are 3 and -2.

31. **(B)** The x-coordinate of the vertex is $-\dfrac{b}{2a} = -\dfrac{4}{4} = -1$. The equation of the axis of symmetry is therefore $x = -1$.

32. **(C)** $\sin\dfrac{A}{a} = \sin\dfrac{C}{c}$; $\angle C = 180° - (42° + 57°) = 81°$; $\sin\dfrac{42°}{a} = \sin\dfrac{81°}{67}$; $a = 45$ cm.

33. **(C)** Write as $x = 0.5555555$. Move the decimal one place to the right to get $10x = 5.5555555$. So $10 - x = 5.5555555 - 0.5555555$ yields $9x = 5$ and $x = \dfrac{5}{9}$.

34. **(B)** Multiply by $\dfrac{\pi}{180°}$: $20° = 20°\left(\dfrac{\pi}{180°}\right) = \dfrac{\pi^R}{9}$.

35. **(C)** The sum of the zeros is found by $-\dfrac{b}{a} = -\dfrac{-5}{1} = 5$.

36. **(C)** Graph a complex number using rectangular coordinates by using the real part as the x-coordinate and the imaginary part as the y-coordinate.

37. **(B)** The sample space contains 8 possibilities, 3 of which contain exactly 2 heads. Probability $= \dfrac{3}{8}$.

38. **(B)** $s^3 = 6\left(\dfrac{4\pi r^3}{3}\right)$; $s^3 = 8\pi r^3$; $\dfrac{s^3}{r^3} = 8\pi$; $\dfrac{s}{r} = \sqrt[3]{8\pi}$.

39. **(D)** $d = \sqrt{(4-2)^2 + (-2-3)^2 + (1-5)^2}$
$= \sqrt{(6)^2 + (-5)^2 + (-4)^2}$
$= \sqrt{36 + 25 + 16}$
$= \sqrt{77}$
$\approx 8.7749643 \approx 8.8$

40. **(D)** The period of the graph is 2π and the amplitude is 1. Therefore, you know that the coefficient of sin is 1. In addition, $\dfrac{2\pi}{2} = \pi$, so the graph must be $y = \sin x$.

41. **(A)** Identify the slope of the line shown. Slope $= m = \dfrac{y_2 - y_1}{x_2 - x_1} = \dfrac{1}{2}$. The slope of a line perpendicular to this will have a slope that is the negative reciprocal, or -2. The only line with this slope is (A).

42. **(B)** Complete the square in the equation of the circle: $(x - 2)^2 + (y + 5)^2 = 9$. The center is at $(2, -5)$ and the radius is 3.

43. **(B)** The real part is 4 and the imaginary part is 3, so the modulus is $\sqrt{4^2 + 3^2} = \sqrt{25} = 5$.

44. **(A)** $\dfrac{10\sqrt{96}}{2\sqrt{2}} = \dfrac{10(4\sqrt{6})}{2\sqrt{2}} = \dfrac{40\sqrt{6}}{2\sqrt{2}} = 20\sqrt{3}$

45. **(D)** Set the expression equal to 0, and substitute 2 for x. Then solve for M: $32 - 32 + 2M - 14 = 0$, so $M = 7$.

46. **(C)** The equation is already in vertex form $y = (x - h)^2 + k$, so the vertex is (h, k).

47. **(D)** Draw a graph to represent the angle. Use $y = -1$ because it is in the third quadrant and $r = 2$. Based on the diagram, $x = -\sqrt{3}$ so $\cos\theta = -\dfrac{\sqrt{3}}{2}$.

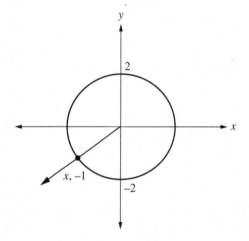

48. **(B)** The range is the spread from the largest value to the least value: $48 - 23 = 25$.

49. **(D)** $(2 + 3i)(2 - 3i) = 4 - 6i + 6i - 9i^2 = i^2 = -1$, so the equation becomes $4 + 9 = 13$.

50. **(C)** The equation of a horizontal line has only one variable. The y-value is constant, but the x-value can be any value, so the equation is $y = -4$.

▬ DIAGNOSE YOUR STRENGTHS AND WEAKNESSES

Check the number of each question answered correctly and "X" the number of each question answered incorrectly.

Algebra and Functions	1	5	7	9	10	11	13	14	15	17	20	Total Number Correct
25 questions												
	22	24	25	26	28	30	31	35	44	45	46	

Trigonometry	3	6	16	21	29	32	34	40	47	Total Number Correct
9 questions										

Coordinate and Three-Dimensional Geometry	4	12	23	38	39	41	42	50	Total Number Correct
8 questions									

Numbers and Operations	2	18	27	33	36	43	49	Total Number Correct
7 questions								

Data Analysis, Statistics, and Probability	8	19	37	48	Total Number Correct
4 questions					

Number of correct answers $- \dfrac{1}{4}$ **(Number of incorrect answers) = Your raw score**

_____ $- \dfrac{1}{4}$ (_____) = _____

Compare your raw score with the approximate SAT Subject Test score below:

	Raw Score	SAT Subject Test Approximate Score
Excellent	43–50	770–800
Very Good	33–43	670–770
Good	27–33	620–670
Above Average	21–27	570–620
Average	11–21	500–570
Below Average	< 11	< 500

PRACTICE TEST 3

Treat this practice test as the actual test and complete it in one 60-minute sitting. Use the following answer sheet to fill in your multiple-choice answers. Once you have completed the practice test:

1. Check your answers using the Answer Key.
2. Review the Answers and Solutions.
3. Fill in the "Diagnose Your Strengths and Weaknesses" sheet, and determine areas that require further preparation.

PRACTICE TEST 3
MATH LEVEL 2

ANSWER SHEET

Tear out this answer sheet and use it to complete the practice test. Determine the BEST answer for each question. Then, fill in the appropriate oval using a No. 2 pencil.

1. (A) (B) (C) (D) (E)	21. (A) (B) (C) (D) (E)	41. (A) (B) (C) (D) (E)
2. (A) (B) (C) (D) (E)	22. (A) (B) (C) (D) (E)	42. (A) (B) (C) (D) (E)
3. (A) (B) (C) (D) (E)	23. (A) (B) (C) (D) (E)	43. (A) (B) (C) (D) (E)
4. (A) (B) (C) (D) (E)	24. (A) (B) (C) (D) (E)	44. (A) (B) (C) (D) (E)
5. (A) (B) (C) (D) (E)	25. (A) (B) (C) (D) (E)	45. (A) (B) (C) (D) (E)
6. (A) (B) (C) (D) (E)	26. (A) (B) (C) (D) (E)	46. (A) (B) (C) (D) (E)
7. (A) (B) (C) (D) (E)	27. (A) (B) (C) (D) (E)	47. (A) (B) (C) (D) (E)
8. (A) (B) (C) (D) (E)	28. (A) (B) (C) (D) (E)	48. (A) (B) (C) (D) (E)
9. (A) (B) (C) (D) (E)	29. (A) (B) (C) (D) (E)	49. (A) (B) (C) (D) (E)
10. (A) (B) (C) (D) (E)	30. (A) (B) (C) (D) (E)	50. (A) (B) (C) (D) (E)
11. (A) (B) (C) (D) (E)	31. (A) (B) (C) (D) (E)	
12. (A) (B) (C) (D) (E)	32. (A) (B) (C) (D) (E)	
13. (A) (B) (C) (D) (E)	33. (A) (B) (C) (D) (E)	
14. (A) (B) (C) (D) (E)	34. (A) (B) (C) (D) (E)	
15. (A) (B) (C) (D) (E)	35. (A) (B) (C) (D) (E)	
16. (A) (B) (C) (D) (E)	36. (A) (B) (C) (D) (E)	
17. (A) (B) (C) (D) (E)	37. (A) (B) (C) (D) (E)	
18. (A) (B) (C) (D) (E)	38. (A) (B) (C) (D) (E)	
19. (A) (B) (C) (D) (E)	39. (A) (B) (C) (D) (E)	
20. (A) (B) (C) (D) (E)	40. (A) (B) (C) (D) (E)	

PRACTICE TEST 3

Time: 60 minutes

Directions: Select the BEST answer for each of the 50 multiple-choice questions. If the exact solution is not one of the five choices, select the answer that is the best approximation. Then, fill in the appropriate oval on the answer sheet.

Notes:

1. A calculator will be needed to answer some of the questions on the test. Scientific, programmable, and graphing calculators are permitted. It is up to you to determine when and when not to use your calculator.

2. Angles on the Level 2 test are measured in degrees and radians. You need to decide whether your calculator should be set to degree mode or radian mode for a particular question.

3. Figures are drawn as accurately as possible and are intended to help solve some of the test problems. If a figure is not drawn to scale, this will be stated in the problem. All figures lie in a plane unless the problem indicates otherwise.

4. Unless otherwise stated, the domain of a function f is assumed to be the set of real numbers x for which the value of the function, $f(x)$, is a real number.

5. Reference information that may be useful in answering some of the test questions can be found below.

Reference Information	
Right circular cone with radius r and height h:	Volume $= \dfrac{1}{3}\pi r^2 h$
Right circular cone with circumference of base c and slant height ℓ:	Lateral Area $= \dfrac{1}{2}c\ell$
Sphere with radius r:	Volume $= \dfrac{4}{3}\pi r^3$ Surface Area $= 4\pi r^2$
Pyramid with base area B and height h:	Volume $= \dfrac{1}{3}Bh$

PRACTICE TEST 3 QUESTIONS

1. Which equation describes the line connecting the points shown?

   (A) $y + 2 = -\dfrac{3}{4}(x - 6)$

   (B) $y - 6 = \dfrac{3}{4}(x + 2)$

   (C) $y - 3 = -3(x + 4)$

   (D) $y - 2 = -\dfrac{3}{4}(x + 6)$

   (E) $y + 4 = (x - 3)$

USE THIS SPACE AS SCRATCH PAPER

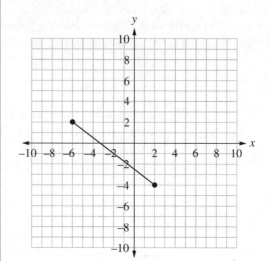

2. For $f(x) = 2x^2 + 4$, $g(x) = 1$, and $h\{(1, 3), (2, 1), (3, 1)\}$,

   (A) f is the only function
   (B) g is the only function
   (C) f and g are the only functions
   (D) g and h are the only functions
   (E) f, g, and h are all functions

3. What is the length of b in the triangle below?

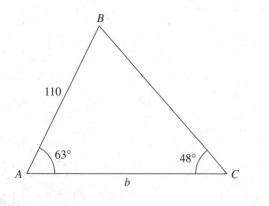

   (A) 70 cm
   (B) 86 cm
   (C) 93 cm
   (D) 103 cm
   (E) 138 cm

GO ON TO THE NEXT PAGE

4. What is the median of the frequency distribution shown?

   (A) 0
   (B) 2
   (C) 3
   (D) 5
   (E) 4

USE THIS SPACE AS SCRATCH PAPER

Data Value	Frequency
0	2
1	6
2	4
3	8
4	5
5	1

5. If $f(x) = 3x - 1$ and $g(x) = 2^x$, $f(g(2)) =$

   (A) 5
   (B) 11
   (C) 25
   (D) 48
   (E) 64

6. If $g(x) = 5x + 3$ and $g(f(x)) = x$, then $f(3) =$

   (A) 0
   (B) 3
   (C) 5
   (D) 11
   (E) 18

7. If the repeating decimal 1.0424242 is written as a fraction in lowest terms, what is the numerator?

   (A) 9
   (B) 42
   (C) 104
   (D) 990
   (E) 1032

8. What is the period of the function $y = \sin\dfrac{1}{4}x$?

   (A) $\dfrac{\pi}{4}$

   (B) $\dfrac{\pi}{8}$

   (C) 4π

   (D) 8π

   (E) $\dfrac{\pi}{2}$

9. What is the range of the function $f(x) = -2x^2 - 4x + 1$?

   (A) $x \le 6$
   (B) $x \ge 0$
   (C) $y \ge 3$
   (D) $y \le 3$
   (E) all real numbers

GO ON TO THE NEXT PAGE

10. A point has rectangular coordinates (3, 4). The polar coordinates are (5, θ). What is θ?

    (A) 31°
    (B) 39°
    (C) 53°
    (D) 68°
    (E) 75°

11. What is the distance between two points in space, $P(3, 2, 1)$ and $R(-2, 0, 1)$?

    (A) 2.7
    (B) 3.5
    (C) 4.4
    (D) 5.4
    (E) 9.2

12. If $f(x) = ax^2 + bx + c$, $f(1) = 7$ and $f(-1) = -1$, then $a + c =$

    (A) −2
    (B) 1
    (C) 3
    (D) 5
    (E) 6

13. What is sin 300° in terms of θ_r?

    (A) −sin 60°
    (B) −sin 40°
    (C) −sin 20°
    (D) sin 30°
    (E) sin 40°

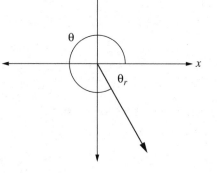

14. Find the matrix equation that represents the system
    $$\begin{cases} 3x + 1 = 2y \\ 4y + x = 8 \end{cases}$$

    (A) $\begin{pmatrix} -1 \\ 8 \end{pmatrix}(x \quad y) = \begin{pmatrix} 3 & 1 \\ 4 & 1 \end{pmatrix}$

    (B) $\begin{pmatrix} 3 & -2 \\ 1 & 4 \end{pmatrix}\begin{pmatrix} x \\ y \end{pmatrix} = \begin{pmatrix} -1 \\ 8 \end{pmatrix}$

    (C) $\begin{pmatrix} 3 & 1 \\ 4 & 1 \end{pmatrix}\begin{pmatrix} x \\ y \end{pmatrix} = \begin{pmatrix} 2 \\ 8 \end{pmatrix}$

    (D) $\begin{pmatrix} -2 & y \\ 4 & y \end{pmatrix}\begin{pmatrix} 3x \\ x \end{pmatrix} = \begin{pmatrix} -1 \\ 8 \end{pmatrix}$

    (E) $\begin{pmatrix} x \\ y \end{pmatrix}\begin{pmatrix} 2 & 3 \\ 4 & 1 \end{pmatrix} = \begin{pmatrix} 1 \\ 8 \end{pmatrix}$

GO ON TO THE NEXT PAGE

15. If $f(x) = x^3 - 2$, then the inverse of $f =$

(A) $\sqrt[3]{x+2}$

(B) $x^3 + 2$

(C) $\sqrt[3]{x-2}$

(D) $\dfrac{1}{x^3 - 2}$

(E) $\dfrac{2}{\sqrt[3]{x}}$

16. The slope of a line through points $A(-1, 3)$ and $B(-4, 2)$ is

(A) -1

(B) $-\dfrac{1}{4}$

(C) $\dfrac{1}{3}$

(D) 2

(E) 3

17. Which equation describes a line that is parallel to the line shown?

(A) $3y - 2x = 10$

(B) $y + 2x = 6$

(C) $2y - 3x = 4$

(D) $y - x = \dfrac{2}{3}$

(E) $3y + x = 2$

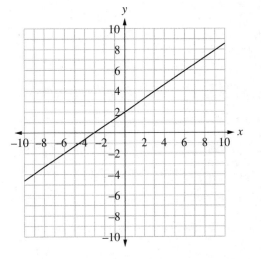

18. What is the axis of symmetry of the function $y = x^2 - 4x + 2$?

(A) $x = \dfrac{1}{2}$

(B) $x = \dfrac{2}{3}$

(C) $x = 2$

(D) $x = 4$

(E) $x = 6$

GO ON TO THE NEXT PAGE

19. The slope of line $3y - 9x + 12 = 0$ is

    (A) −4
    (B) $-\dfrac{1}{3}$
    (C) $\dfrac{1}{4}$
    (D) 2
    (E) 3

20. If $\sin x = 0.4818$, what is $\csc x$?

    (A) −1.48
    (B) −0.99
    (C) 0.52
    (D) 1.48
    (E) 2.08

21. The slope of the line perpendicular to line $4x + y - 8 = 0$ is

    (A) −4
    (B) −2
    (C) $-\dfrac{1}{2}$
    (D) $\dfrac{1}{4}$
    (E) 4

22. Which is the center of the circle $(x + 2)^2 + (y - 12)^2 = 36$?

    (A) (6, 6)
    (B) (−2, 12)
    (C) (−6, −6)
    (D) (2, −12)
    (E) (2, 6)

23. What is the radius of circle $x^2 + y^2 - 4x = 6y - 8$?

    (A) $\sqrt{2}$
    (B) 3
    (C) 5
    (D) $2\sqrt{2}$
    (E) $\sqrt{5}$

24. The y-intercept of the line through two points whose coordinates are (−1, −5) and (2, 4) is

    (A) −2
    (B) $-\dfrac{1}{2}$
    (C) $\dfrac{1}{2}$
    (D) 3
    (E) 5

GO ON TO THE NEXT PAGE

25. Point *y* is a complex number shown on the graph. Which point could be *iy*?

    (A) *A*
    (B) *B*
    (C) *C*
    (D) *D*
    (E) *E*

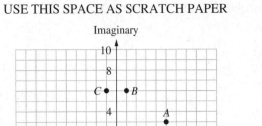

26. A student tosses a coin three times. What is the probability that three heads will appear?

    (A) $\dfrac{1}{4}$

    (B) $\dfrac{3}{8}$

    (C) $\dfrac{1}{2}$

    (D) $\dfrac{1}{8}$

    (E) $\dfrac{3}{4}$

27. The coordinates of the vertex of the parabola whose equation is $y = x^2 - 4x - 5$ are

    (A) $(2, -9)$
    (B) $(1, -4)$
    (C) $(-5, -2)$
    (D) $(8, -5)$
    (E) $(4, -17)$

28. Which function below could be represented by the graph?

    (A) $y = \dfrac{1}{8} \sin \pi x$

    (B) $y = 8 \sin 2\pi$

    (C) $y = 3 \sin \left(2x + \dfrac{\pi}{4}\right)$

    (D) $y = \sin \left(x + \dfrac{\pi}{8}\right)$

    (E) $y = \dfrac{1}{3} \sin \dfrac{\pi}{4}$

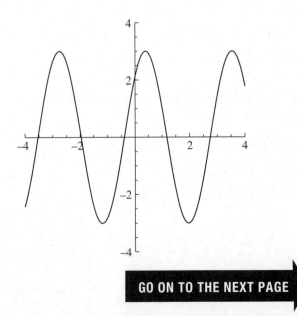

GO ON TO THE NEXT PAGE

29. Find the zeros of $y = 2x^2 + 3x - 2$.

    (A) $2, 3$

    (B) $-2, \dfrac{1}{2}$

    (C) $-\dfrac{3}{2}, \dfrac{1}{2}$

    (D) $-1, 2$

    (E) $-\dfrac{1}{2}, 1$

30. The segment of the line $y = -x + 1$ that lies in quadrant I is rotated about the y-axis to form a cone. What is the volume of the cone?

    (A) π

    (B) 3π

    (C) $\dfrac{\pi}{2}$

    (D) $\dfrac{\pi}{3}$

    (E) $\dfrac{2\pi}{3}$

31. The range of the function $f = \{(x, y): y = 2x^2 + 8x + 1\}$ is

    (A) $\{y : y \geq 2\}$
    (B) $\{y : y \geq 0\}$
    (C) $\{y : y \geq -7\}$
    (D) $\{y : y \leq -2\}$
    (E) $\{y : y \leq -7\}$

32. Which is the period of $y = \dfrac{1}{2} \sin\left(\dfrac{\pi x}{3}\right)$?

    (A) 2π
    (B) 3
    (C) $\dfrac{2\pi}{3}$
    (D) 6
    (E) $\dfrac{\pi}{3}$

33. The equation of the axis of symmetry of the function $y = x^2 - 4x + 5$ is

    (A) $x = \dfrac{1}{2}$

    (B) $x = -2$

    (C) $x = \dfrac{2}{3}$

    (D) $x = 2$

    (E) $x = -\dfrac{4}{5}$

USE THIS SPACE AS SCRATCH PAPER

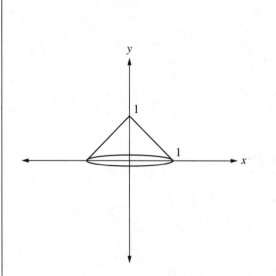

GO ON TO THE NEXT PAGE

34. What is $\dfrac{3-i}{2-3i}$ in standard form?

    (A) $\dfrac{3}{2} - \dfrac{1}{3}i$

    (B) $\dfrac{13}{16}i$

    (C) $\dfrac{9}{13} + \dfrac{7}{13}i$

    (D) $(9+7i)$

    (E) $(2+3i)$

35. What is the length of the longest segment with end-points at vertices of the rectangular solid?

    (A) 17.0 cm
    (B) 10.4 cm
    (C) 8.6 cm
    (D) 4.4 cm
    (E) 3.1 cm

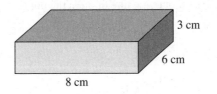

3 cm

6 cm

8 cm

36. If a prime number is less than 17, what is the probability that it is also less than 11?

    (A) $\dfrac{1}{4}$

    (B) $\dfrac{1}{3}$

    (C) $\dfrac{2}{3}$

    (D) $\dfrac{3}{4}$

    (E) $\dfrac{2}{5}$

37. If $x > 0$, what is the approximate value of x in the equation $4 + \log_3(7x) = 10$?

    (A) 21
    (B) 42
    (C) 73
    (D) 104
    (E) 126

38. A jar contains 3 black marbles and 2 white marbles. Two marbles are drawn from the jar at random. What is the probability that both marbles are black?

    (A) 0.1
    (B) 0.2
    (C) 0.3
    (D) 0.4
    (E) 0.5

GO ON TO THE NEXT PAGE

39. Which equation best describes the graph?

    (A) $y = \sqrt{2}x$

    (B) $y = |x + 2|$

    (C) $y = 4x^5 + 2x^3 - 3x$

    (D) $y = \dfrac{(x-2)^2}{2} + \dfrac{(y+1)^2}{4}$

    (E) $y = \sin(-2x + 1)$

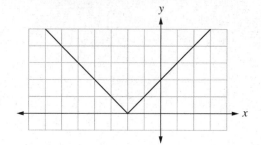

40. What is the y-intercept of the line through the points $(3, -1)$ and $(7, 5)$?

    (A) $\dfrac{-1}{2}$

    (B) $\dfrac{1}{2}$

    (C) 2

    (D) 3

    (E) $\dfrac{21}{2}$

41. What are the rectangular coordinates of a point with polar coordinates $(5, 30°)$?

    (A) $(2.5, 4.3)$

    (B) $(2.8, 4.4)$

    (C) $(25, 30)$

    (D) $(4.3, 2.5)$

    (E) $(5.3, 12.5)$

42. If $f(x)$ is $3x + 2$, what is $f^{-1}(x)$?

    (A) $f^{-1}(x) = 2x + 3$

    (B) $f^{-1}(x) = x + \dfrac{2}{3}$

    (C) $f^{-1}(x) = \dfrac{x}{3} - \dfrac{2}{3}$

    (D) $f^{-1}(x) = 5x$

    (E) $f^{-1}(x) = \dfrac{2}{3}x + \dfrac{3}{2}$

43. If $\dfrac{2x - y}{x} = 6$, what is the value of $\dfrac{x}{y}$?

    (A) $-\dfrac{1}{6}$

    (B) $-\dfrac{1}{4}$

    (C) $-\dfrac{1}{2}$

    (D) $\dfrac{1}{6}$

    (E) $\dfrac{1}{4}$

GO ON TO THE NEXT PAGE

44. If $|2x+1| > 2$, which of the following quantities is a possible value of x?

    (A) $x = -2$
    (B) $x = -1$
    (C) $x = 0$
    (D) $x = \dfrac{1}{8}$
    (E) $x = \dfrac{1}{4}$

USE THIS SPACE AS SCRATCH PAPER

45. $\tan^{-1}(\tan 96) =$

    (A) -84
    (B) -10
    (C) -0.95
    (D) 10
    (E) 84

46. How many 3-player squads can be selected from a group of 32 players?

    (A) 96
    (B) 192
    (C) 2631
    (D) 4960
    (E) 7893

47. A family has three pets. The pets are either cats or dogs. What is the probability that at least one pet is a cat?

    (A) 0.050
    (B) 0.250
    (C) 0.500
    (D) 0.875
    (E) 0.920

48. What is $\dfrac{x^2 - x - 6}{x^2 + x - 2}$?

    (A) $\dfrac{x-1}{x-3}$
    (B) $\dfrac{(x+2)}{(x-3)}$
    (C) $\dfrac{(x-3)}{(x-1)}$
    (D) $2x + 4$
    (E) $2x^2 - 8$

GO ON TO THE NEXT PAGE

49. Alexa invests $1000 in an account that pays 4.0% compounded quarterly. How much money will Alexa have at the end of 5 years?

    (A) $1040.00
    (B) $1056.44
    (C) $1144.20
    (D) $1220.19
    (E) $1245.00

50. Solve for x in the equation $x^2 = x + 20$.

    (A) 2 or 10
    (B) −2 or 4
    (C) −5 or 4
    (D) −4 or 5
    (E) −2 or 3

USE THIS SPACE AS SCRATCH PAPER

STOP

IF YOU FINISH BEFORE TIME IS CALLED, YOU MAY CHECK YOUR WORK ON THIS TEST ONLY.
DO NOT TURN TO ANY OTHER TEST IN THIS BOOK.

ANSWER KEY

1. D	11. D	21. D	31. C	41. D
2. E	12. C	22. B	32. D	42. C
3. E	13. A	23. E	33. D	43. B
4. C	14. B	24. A	34. C	44. A
5. B	15. A	25. C	35. B	45. A
6. A	16. C	26. D	36. C	46. D
7. E	17. A	27. A	37. D	47. D
8. D	18. C	28. C	38. C	48. C
9. D	19. E	29. B	39. B	49. D
10. C	20. E	30. D	40. A	50. D

ANSWERS AND EXPLANATIONS

1. **(D)** First find the slope: $m = \dfrac{2-(-4)}{-6-2} = -\dfrac{6}{8} = -\dfrac{3}{4}$.
Then use the point $(-6, 2)$ along with the slope to write the point-slope equation $y - 2 = -\dfrac{3}{4}(x+6)$.

2. **(E)** For each value of x, there is only one value for y in each of f, g, and h.

3. **(E)** $\sin \dfrac{C}{c} = \sin \dfrac{B}{b}$; $\angle C = 180° - (63° + 48°) = 69°$; $\dfrac{\sin 48°}{110} = \dfrac{\sin 69°}{b}$; $b = 138$ cm.

4. **(C)** There are a total of 26 data values. The median is the mean of the 13th and 14th values. These values are both 3, so the median is 3.

5. **(B)** $g(2) = 2^2 = 4$; $f(4) = 3(4) - 1 = 11$

6. **(A)** Since $f(3)$ implies that $x = 3$, $g(f(3)) = 3$. Therefore, $g(f(3)) = 5(f(3)) + 3 = 3$. So $f(3) = 0$.

7. **(E)** Write as $x = 1.0424242$. Move the decimal three places to the right to get $1000x = 1042.424242$, and one place to get $10x = 10.42424242$. Then $1000x - 10x = 1042.424242 - 10.42424242$, which yields $990x = 1032$ and $x = \dfrac{1032}{990}$.

8. **(D)** The period is $\dfrac{2\pi}{\frac{1}{4}} = 2\pi \cdot 4 = 8\pi$.

9. **(D)** Plot the graph $-2x^2 - 4x + 1$, and find its vertex at $(-1, 3)$. The parabola opens downward so the range of $f(x)$ is $(-\infty, 3]$.

10. **(C)**

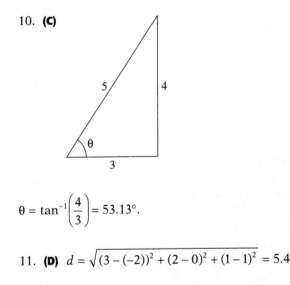

$\theta = \tan^{-1}\left(\dfrac{4}{3}\right) = 53.13°$.

11. **(D)** $d = \sqrt{(3-(-2))^2 + (2-0)^2 + (1-1)^2} = 5.4$

12. **(C)** $f(1) = a + b + c = 7$ and $f(-1) = a - b + c = -1$. Adding these yields $f(1) + f(-1) = 2a + 2c = 6$, so $a + c = 3$.

13. **(A)** $\theta_r = 360° - 300° = 60°$. The sine is negative in quadrant IV, so $\sin 300° = -\sin 60°$.

14. **(B)** Write the system in standard form $\begin{cases} 3x - 2y = -1 \\ x + 4y = 8 \end{cases}$. Use the coefficients $\begin{pmatrix} 3 & -2 \\ 1 & 4 \end{pmatrix}$, variables $\begin{pmatrix} x \\ y \end{pmatrix}$, and constants $\begin{pmatrix} -1 \\ 8 \end{pmatrix}$ to find the matrix equation.

15. **(A)** Let $y = x^3 - 2$. To get the inverse, interchange x and y, and solve for y. $x = y^3 - 2$. $y^3 = x + 2$. $y = \sqrt[3]{x + 2}$.

16. **(C)** Slope $= \dfrac{3 - 2}{-1 - (-4)} = \dfrac{1}{3}$

17. **(A)** The slope of the line on the graph is $\dfrac{2}{3}$. Parallel lines have the same slope. Rewrite each equation in the slope-intercept form to evaluate the slope. For Choice A, $3y - 2x = 10$ becomes $3y = 2x + 10$ and then $y = \dfrac{2}{3}x + \dfrac{10}{3}$. This line has a slope of $\dfrac{2}{3}$ and is therefore parallel.

18. **(C)**

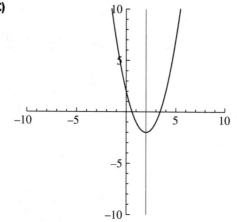

The axis of symmetry is the x-coordinate of the vertex, which is $x = \dfrac{4}{2(1)} = 2$.

19. **(E)** Rewrite the equation in terms of y. $3y = 9x - 12$. $y = 3x - 4$. The slope is 3. Another method is to rewrite the equation in standard form. $-9x + 3y = -12$, $m = -\left(\dfrac{A}{B}\right) = -\left(\dfrac{-9}{3}\right) = 3$.

20. **(E)** $\csc x = \dfrac{1}{\sin x} = \dfrac{1}{0.4818} = 2.08$.

21. **(D)** Rewrite the equation in terms of y. $y = -4x + 8$. The slope of the line is -4. The slope of a perpendicular line is the negative reciprocal, which is $\dfrac{1}{4}$.

22. **(B)** Identify the coordinates from the equation. $(x + 2)$ indicates that the x-coordinate is -2. $(y - 12)$ indicates that the y-coordinate is 12.

23. **(E)** Complete the square in the equation of the circle: $(x - 2)^2 + (y - 3)^2 = 5$. The center is at $(2, 3)$ and the radius is $\sqrt{5}$.

24. **(A)** The slope of the line is $\dfrac{-5 - 4}{-1 - 2} = 3$, so the point-slope equation is $y - 4 = 3(x - 2)$. Solve for y to get $y = 3x - 2$. The y-intercept of the line is -2.

25. **(C)** $y = 6 + i$, so $iy = -1 + 6i$, which is point C.

26. **(D)** The sample space contains 8 possibilities, only one of which contains three heads. Probability $= \dfrac{1}{8}$.

27. **(A)** The x coordinate of the vertex is $x = -\dfrac{b}{2a} = -\dfrac{-4}{2} = 2$ and the y-coordinate is $y = (2)^2 - 4(2) - 5 = -9$. Therefore, the vertex is the point $(2, -9)$.

28. **(C)** The period of the graph is π and the amplitude is 3. Therefore, you know that the coefficient of sin is 3. The phase shift is $\dfrac{\pi}{4}$ units to the left.

29. **(B)** $2x^2 + 3x - 2 = (2x - 1)(x + 2) = 0$, so the zeros are $\dfrac{1}{2}$ and -2.

30. **(D)** The radius of the base is 1 and the height is 1. $V = \dfrac{1}{3}\pi(1)^1(1) = \dfrac{1}{3}\pi$.

31. **(C)** The vertex is $x = -\dfrac{b}{2a} = -\dfrac{8}{4} = -2$ and $y = 2(-2)^2 + 8(-2) + 1 = -7$. Because $a = 2 > 0$, the parabola opens upward, so the range is $\{y: y \geq -7\}$.

32. **(D)** Rewrite as $y = \dfrac{1}{2}\sin\left(\dfrac{\pi}{3}\right)x$. Period $= \dfrac{2\pi}{\dfrac{\pi}{3}} = 6$.

33. **(D)** The x-coordinate of the vertex is $-\dfrac{b}{2a} = -\dfrac{-4}{2} = 2$. The equation of the axis of symmetry is therefore $x = 2$.

34. **(C)** $\dfrac{3 - i}{2 - 3i} = \dfrac{(3 - i)(2 + 3i)}{2 - 3i(2 + 3i)} = \dfrac{9 + 7i}{13} = \dfrac{9}{13} + \dfrac{7}{13}i$

35. **(B)** Find the length of the diagonal: $\sqrt{8^2 + 6^2 + 3^2} \approx 10.4$.

36. **(C)** There are 6 prime numbers less than 17. Of those, four are less than 11, so the probability is $\frac{4}{6}$, or $\frac{2}{3}$.

37. **(D)** $\text{Log}_3(7x) = 6$ becomes $3^6 = 7x$. Divide both sides of the equation by 7: $x = \frac{3^6}{7}$, which is approximately 104.

38. **(C)** $P(\text{two black marbles}) = \frac{3}{5} \cdot \frac{2}{4} = \frac{6}{20} = \frac{3}{10} = 0.3$.

39. **(B)** A graph of this shape generally represents an absolute value. To confirm, test positive and negative values of x.

40. **(A)** The slope of the line is $m = \frac{-1-5}{3-7} = \frac{-6}{-4} = \frac{3}{2}$. The point slope equation is $y - 5 = \frac{3}{2}(x - 7)$. Solve for y to get $y = \frac{3}{2}x - \frac{11}{2}$ so the y-intercept is $\frac{-11}{4}$.

41. **(D)** $(x, y) = (5 \cos 30°, 5 \sin 30°) = (4.3, 2.5)$

42. **(C)** Interchange the x and y, and solve: $y = 3x + 2$ becomes $x = 3y + 2$. Then $3y = x - 2$ so $y = \frac{x}{3} - \frac{2}{3}$.

43. **(B)** Multiply through by x to get $2x - y = 6x$. Then combine x terms, $-y = 4x$. Divide both sides by 4 and y to get $-\frac{1}{4} = \frac{x}{y}$.

44. **(A)** Let $2x + 1$ be positive, such as $2x + 1 > 2$ and $2x > 1$ so $x > \frac{1}{2}$. Let $2x + 1$ be negative such that $2x + 1 < -2$ and $2x < -3$ so $x < -\frac{3}{2}$. Choose a value that lies in one of the ranges.

45. **(A)** With your calculator set to degree mode, enter 2nd $\tan^{-1}(\tan 96)$ to find the answer.

46. **(D)** The problem involves a combination because order does not matter. To find the answer, enter the values for $_{32}C_3$ in you calculator to solve. Or find the solution as $C(3, 32) = \frac{32!}{3!(32-3)!}$.

47. **(D)** The probability that at least one pet is a cat is (1 – the probability that all three pets are dogs), which is $1 - (0.5)^3 = 0.875$.

48. **(C)** Factor the numerator and the denominator, and then cancel. $\frac{x^2 - x - 6}{x^2 + x - 2} = \frac{(x+2)(x-3)}{(x+2)(x-1)} = \frac{(x-3)}{(x-1)}$.

49. **(D)** $A = P\left(1 + \frac{r}{n}\right)^{nt} = 1000\left(1 + \frac{0.04}{4}\right)^{4 \times 5} = 1220.19$

50. **(D)** Rewrite in standard form and then factor. $x^2 - x - 20 = 0$, $(x + 4)(x - 5) = 0$, so $x = -4$ or 5.

▮ DIAGNOSE YOUR STRENGTHS AND WEAKNESSES

Check the number of each question answered correctly and "X" the number of each question answered incorrectly.

Algebra and Functions	1	2	5	6	9	12	15	16	18	19	21	24	27	Total Number Correct
25 questions														
	29	31	33	37	39	40	42	43	44	48	49	50		

Trigonometry	3	8	13	20	28	32	45	Total Number Correct
7 questions								

Coordinate and Three-Dimensional Geometry	10	11	17	22	23	30	35	41	Total Number Correct
8 questions									

Numbers and Operations	7	14	25	34	46	Total Number Correct
5 questions						

Data Analysis, Statistics, and Probability	4	26	36	38	47	Total Number Correct
5 questions						

Number of correct answers $-\dfrac{1}{4}$ **(Number of incorrect answers) = Your raw score**

_____ $-\dfrac{1}{4}$ (_____) = _____

Compare your raw score with the approximate SAT Subject Test score below:

	Raw Score	SAT Subject Test Approximate Score
Excellent	43–50	770–800
Very Good	33–43	670–770
Good	27–33	620–670
Above Average	21–27	570–620
Average	11–21	500–570
Below Average	< 11	< 500

PRACTICE TEST 4

Treat this practice test as the actual test and complete it in one 60-minute sitting. Use the following answer sheet to fill in your multiple-choice answers. Once you have completed the practice test:

1. Check your answers using the Answer Key.
2. Review the Answers and Solutions.
3. Fill in the "Diagnose Your Strengths and Weaknesses" sheet, and determine areas that require further preparation.

PRACTICE TEST 4

MATH LEVEL 2

ANSWER SHEET

Tear out this answer sheet and use it to complete the practice test. Determine the BEST answer for each question. Then, fill in the appropriate oval using a No. 2 pencil.

1. Ⓐ Ⓑ Ⓒ Ⓓ Ⓔ	21. Ⓐ Ⓑ Ⓒ Ⓓ Ⓔ	41. Ⓐ Ⓑ Ⓒ Ⓓ Ⓔ
2. Ⓐ Ⓑ Ⓒ Ⓓ Ⓔ	22. Ⓐ Ⓑ Ⓒ Ⓓ Ⓔ	42. Ⓐ Ⓑ Ⓒ Ⓓ Ⓔ
3. Ⓐ Ⓑ Ⓒ Ⓓ Ⓔ	23. Ⓐ Ⓑ Ⓒ Ⓓ Ⓔ	43. Ⓐ Ⓑ Ⓒ Ⓓ Ⓔ
4. Ⓐ Ⓑ Ⓒ Ⓓ Ⓔ	24. Ⓐ Ⓑ Ⓒ Ⓓ Ⓔ	44. Ⓐ Ⓑ Ⓒ Ⓓ Ⓔ
5. Ⓐ Ⓑ Ⓒ Ⓓ Ⓔ	25. Ⓐ Ⓑ Ⓒ Ⓓ Ⓔ	45. Ⓐ Ⓑ Ⓒ Ⓓ Ⓔ
6. Ⓐ Ⓑ Ⓒ Ⓓ Ⓔ	26. Ⓐ Ⓑ Ⓒ Ⓓ Ⓔ	46. Ⓐ Ⓑ Ⓒ Ⓓ Ⓔ
7. Ⓐ Ⓑ Ⓒ Ⓓ Ⓔ	27. Ⓐ Ⓑ Ⓒ Ⓓ Ⓔ	47. Ⓐ Ⓑ Ⓒ Ⓓ Ⓔ
8. Ⓐ Ⓑ Ⓒ Ⓓ Ⓔ	28. Ⓐ Ⓑ Ⓒ Ⓓ Ⓔ	48. Ⓐ Ⓑ Ⓒ Ⓓ Ⓔ
9. Ⓐ Ⓑ Ⓒ Ⓓ Ⓔ	29. Ⓐ Ⓑ Ⓒ Ⓓ Ⓔ	49. Ⓐ Ⓑ Ⓒ Ⓓ Ⓔ
10. Ⓐ Ⓑ Ⓒ Ⓓ Ⓔ	30. Ⓐ Ⓑ Ⓒ Ⓓ Ⓔ	50. Ⓐ Ⓑ Ⓒ Ⓓ Ⓔ
11. Ⓐ Ⓑ Ⓒ Ⓓ Ⓔ	31. Ⓐ Ⓑ Ⓒ Ⓓ Ⓔ	
12. Ⓐ Ⓑ Ⓒ Ⓓ Ⓔ	32. Ⓐ Ⓑ Ⓒ Ⓓ Ⓔ	
13. Ⓐ Ⓑ Ⓒ Ⓓ Ⓔ	33. Ⓐ Ⓑ Ⓒ Ⓓ Ⓔ	
14. Ⓐ Ⓑ Ⓒ Ⓓ Ⓔ	34. Ⓐ Ⓑ Ⓒ Ⓓ Ⓔ	
15. Ⓐ Ⓑ Ⓒ Ⓓ Ⓔ	35. Ⓐ Ⓑ Ⓒ Ⓓ Ⓔ	
16. Ⓐ Ⓑ Ⓒ Ⓓ Ⓔ	36. Ⓐ Ⓑ Ⓒ Ⓓ Ⓔ	
17. Ⓐ Ⓑ Ⓒ Ⓓ Ⓔ	37. Ⓐ Ⓑ Ⓒ Ⓓ Ⓔ	
18. Ⓐ Ⓑ Ⓒ Ⓓ Ⓔ	38. Ⓐ Ⓑ Ⓒ Ⓓ Ⓔ	
19. Ⓐ Ⓑ Ⓒ Ⓓ Ⓔ	39. Ⓐ Ⓑ Ⓒ Ⓓ Ⓔ	
20. Ⓐ Ⓑ Ⓒ Ⓓ Ⓔ	40. Ⓐ Ⓑ Ⓒ Ⓓ Ⓔ	

PRACTICE TEST 4

Time: 60 minutes

Directions: Select the BEST answer for each of the 50 multiple-choice questions. If the exact solution is not one of the five choices, select the answer that is the best approximation. Then, fill in the appropriate oval on the answer sheet.

Notes:

1. A calculator will be needed to answer some of the questions on the test. Scientific, programmable, and graphing calculators are permitted. It is up to you to determine when and when not to use your calculator.
2. Angles on the Level 2 test are measured in degrees and radians. You need to decide whether your calculator should be set to degree mode or radian mode for a particular question.
3. Figures are drawn as accurately as possible and are intended to help solve some of the test problems. If a figure is not drawn to scale, this will be stated in the problem. All figures lie in a plane unless the problem indicates otherwise.
4. Unless otherwise stated, the domain of a function f is assumed to be the set of real numbers x for which the value of the function, $f(x)$, is a real number.
5. Reference information that may be useful in answering some of the test questions can be found below.

Reference Information
Right circular cone with radius r and height h: Volume $= \dfrac{1}{3}\pi r^2 h$
Right circular cone with circumference of base c and slant height ℓ: Lateral Area $= \dfrac{1}{2}c\ell$
Sphere with radius r: Volume $= \dfrac{4}{3}\pi r^3$ Surface Area $= 4\pi r^2$
Pyramid with base area B and height h: Volume $= \dfrac{1}{3}Bh$

PRACTICE TEST 4 QUESTIONS

1. What is the domain of $f(x) = \sqrt{7 - 2x}$?

   (A) $(-\infty, 0)$
   (B) $(-\infty, 3.5)$
   (C) $(-\infty, 7)$
   (D) $(3.5, \infty)$
   (E) all real numbers

2. If $f(x) = 2x^2 + bx$, then $f(b) =$

   (A) b
   (B) $2b^2$
   (C) $3b^2$
   (D) $b^2 - b$
   (E) 0

3. What is the smallest distance between point $(5, -5)$ and a point on the circumference of the circle described by $(x - 2)^2 + (y + 1)^2 = 9$?

   (A) 2
   (B) 3
   (C) 4
   (D) 5
   (E) 6

4. $\log_{\frac{3}{2}} \dfrac{27}{8} =$

   (A) $\dfrac{2}{3}$

   (B) 2
   (C) 3

   (D) $\dfrac{3}{2}$

   (E) 9

5. Which of the following lines are vertical asymptotes of the graph of $y = \dfrac{x + 4}{x^2 + 3x - 4}$?

   I. $x = -4$
   II. $x = 0$
   III. $x = 1$

   (A) I only
   (B) II only
   (C) III only
   (D) I and III
   (E) II and III

6. The lines $x - 2y = 6$ and $ky + 4x = 8$ are perpendicular when $k =$

   (A) 0
   (B) 1
   (C) 2
   (D) 3
   (E) 6

7. The vertex angle of an isosceles triangle is 40°. If the length of the base is 8 centimeters, what is the perimeter of the triangle?

   (A) 35.09 cm
   (B) 31.39 cm
   (C) 23.39 cm
   (D) 12.68 cm
   (E) 11.70 cm

8. What are the coordinates of the vertex of the parabola whose equation is $y = 3x^2 + 6x - 1$?

   (A) $(-1, 10)$
   (B) $(-3, -6)$
   (C) $(1, 3)$
   (D) $(-1, -4)$
   (E) $(3, 6)$

9. The slope of the linear function, f, is $\frac{1}{2}$. If $f(2) = 0$ and $f(6) = n$, what is n?

   (A) $-\frac{1}{2}$

   (B) $\frac{1}{2}$

   (C) 2
   (D) 4
   (E) 8

10. What is the radius of a sphere with the center at the origin that passes through the point $(1, 3, 5)$?

    (A) 2.25
    (B) 3
    (C) 3.51
    (D) 5.92
    (E) 6.03

11. What is the length of the major axis of the ellipse whose equation is $25x^2 + 9y^2 = 225$?

    (A) 3
    (B) 5
    (C) 6
    (D) 10
    (E) 25

GO ON TO THE NEXT PAGE

USE THIS SPACE AS SCRATCH PAPER

12. Which of the following is a solution to $2x^2 - 3x < 2$?

(A) $-\dfrac{3}{2} < x < 3$

(B) $-\dfrac{1}{2} < x < 2$

(C) $-1 < x < \dfrac{3}{2}$

(D) $0 < x$

(E) $x < -\dfrac{1}{2}$ or $x > 2$

13. The mean, standard deviation, and a particular data value from an experiment are listed in the table. Which single data value has the highest z-score?

(A) A
(B) B
(C) C
(D) D
(E) E

Trial	Mean	Standard Deviation	Single Data Value
A	124	12	134
B	168	15	180
C	146	8	152
D	110	6	121
E	195	20	202

14. How can $(2x^{-1}y^2)^2$ be expressed with only positive exponents?

(A) $\dfrac{4y^4}{x^2}$

(B) $4y^4 - x$

(C) $\sqrt{xy^2}$

(D) $\dfrac{y^2}{2x}$

(E) $\dfrac{2x}{y^2}$

15. Evaluate $\tan^{-1}(\sin 80°)$.

(A) 9.9
(B) 23.6
(C) 44.6
(D) 75.0
(E) 98.5

16. What is the 9th term of an arithmetic sequence that begins with 11 and has a common difference of 4?

(A) 32
(B) 36
(C) 39
(D) 43
(E) 46

GO ON TO THE NEXT PAGE

17. The polar coordinates of point P are $(3, 260°)$. The rectangular coordinates of point P are

    (A) $(-0.17, -0.98)$
    (B) $(-0.99, 0.05)$
    (C) $(-0.52, -2.95)$
    (D) $(-5.79, -3.28)$
    (E) $(5.21, 1.05)$

18. To the nearest tenth, the negative zero of $y = 2x^2 + 4x - 1$ is

    (A) -2.5
    (B) -2.2
    (C) -1.8
    (D) -1.5
    (E) -0.2

19. If $x - 2$ is a factor of $2x^3 + 5x^2 + kx - 16$, what is the value of k?

    (A) -10
    (B) -5
    (C) 0
    (D) 8
    (E) 18

20. A package contains 10 marbles, of which 6 are blue. A second package contains 8 marbles, of which 6 are blue. If a marble is drawn at random from each package, what is the probability that neither marble will be blue?

    (A) $\dfrac{1}{18}$

    (B) $\dfrac{1}{9}$

    (C) $\dfrac{9}{20}$

    (D) $\dfrac{1}{10}$

    (E) $\dfrac{1}{3}$

21. Which of the following is perpendicular to the line $y = -2x + 4$?

    (A) $y = -\dfrac{1}{2}x + 4$

    (B) $y = \dfrac{1}{2}x + 4$

    (C) $y = x + 2$
    (D) $y = 2x + 4$
    (E) $y = 2x - 4$

USE THIS SPACE AS SCRATCH PAPER

GO ON TO THE NEXT PAGE

22. $\left(\sqrt[4]{9}\right)^2 =$

(A) $\sqrt{2}$

(B) 3

(C) $2\sqrt{2}$

(D) 12

(E) 20

23. If $f(x) = 5x - 2$, then $f^{-1}(x)$ is

(A) $\dfrac{1}{5x-2}$

(B) $\dfrac{x+2}{5}$

(C) $5x + 2$

(D) $\dfrac{x+5}{2}$

(E) $2x + 5$

24. If $3x + 2y = 8$ and $2x + y = 5$, what is $x + y$?

(A) -1

(B) 0

(C) 3

(D) 5

(E) 13

25. What is the distance from point $(5, 2)$ to line $3x - y = -6$?

(A) $\dfrac{\sqrt{7}}{6}$

(B) $\dfrac{2\sqrt{5}}{3}$

(C) $\dfrac{10\sqrt{5}}{17}$

(D) $\dfrac{19\sqrt{10}}{10}$

(E) $\dfrac{5\sqrt{2}}{3}$

26. If $\log_3 a = \sqrt{2}$ and $\log_5 b = \sqrt{7}$, $ab =$

(A) 5

(B) 71

(C) 129

(D) 334

(E) 460

GO ON TO THE NEXT PAGE

27. $(3x^2 - 2xy)((4y+1) - 6xy) =$

    (A) $24x^2y + 3x^2 - 18x^3y - 10xy^2$
    (B) $12x^2y + 3x^2 - 18x^3y - 8xy^2$
    (C) $18x^3y + 12x^2y^2$
    (D) $12x^2y + 3x^2 - 2xy + 12x^2y^2$
    (E) $12x^2y + 3x^2 - 18x^3y - 8xy^2 - 2xy + 12x^2y^2$

28. If $f(x) = \dfrac{1}{x-4}$ and $g(x) = \dfrac{1}{x}$, $(f \cdot g)(x)$ equals

    (A) $\dfrac{1}{x^2 - 4x}$

    (B) $\dfrac{x}{x-4}$

    (C) $\dfrac{2x-4}{x^2 - 4x}$

    (D) $\dfrac{1}{x^2}$

    (E) $x + \dfrac{1}{4}$

29. The y-intercept of the line that passes through the points $(2, 5)$ and $(-4, 2)$ is

    (A) -2
    (B) -1
    (C) $\dfrac{1}{2}$
    (D) 4
    (E) 6

30. What is the median of the frequency distribution shown below?

Data Value	Frequency
12	1
13	3
14	5
15	12
16	18
17	12
18	8
19	6

    (A) 12
    (B) 14
    (C) 15
    (D) 16
    (E) 19

USE THIS SPACE AS SCRATCH PAPER

GO ON TO THE NEXT PAGE

31. If *a*, *b*, and *c* are positive, with *ab* = 18, *ac* = 24, and *bc* = 12, then *a* + *b* + *c* =

    (A) 9
    (B) 13
    (C) 21
    (D) 28
    (E) 36

32. What is the measure of *BC* in the triangle below?

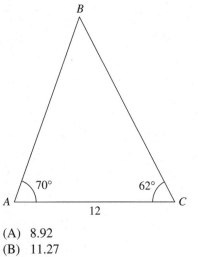

    (A) 8.92
    (B) 11.27
    (C) 13.48
    (D) 15.17
    (E) 18.38

33. How many degrees are equivalent to 22 radians?

    (A) $\dfrac{180°}{\pi}$

    (B) $\dfrac{3960°}{\pi}$

    (C) $\dfrac{3960°}{180\pi}$

    (D) $\pi 3960°$

    (E) $\dfrac{11}{90\pi}$

34. An applicant for a position in a company receives scores from three managers. The applicant needs to have an average score of 7.5 to be considered for a position. If the first manager gave the applicant a score of 7.8 out of 8.0, what is the lowest score the other managers can give for the applicant to be considered for the position?

    (A) 5.5
    (B) 5.8
    (C) 6.2
    (D) 6.7
    (E) 7.5

GO ON TO THE NEXT PAGE

35. What is the measure of ∠A in the triangle below?

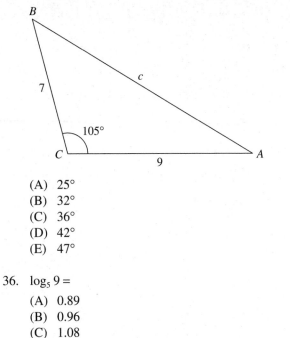

(A) 25°
(B) 32°
(C) 36°
(D) 42°
(E) 47°

36. $\log_5 9 =$
(A) 0.89
(B) 0.96
(C) 1.08
(D) 1.37
(E) 1.45

37. A soccer team has 2 goalies, 7 defensive players, and 8 offensive players. At any given time, there is 1 goalie, 5 defensive players, and 5 offensive players on the field. How many possible combinations of players can be on the field for the team?

(A) 250
(B) 1120
(C) 2352
(D) 9261
(E) 175,616

38. If two fair coins are flipped, what is the probably of one landing heads up and one landing tails up?

(A) $\dfrac{1}{8}$

(B) $\dfrac{1}{6}$

(C) $\dfrac{1}{4}$

(D) $\dfrac{1}{3}$

(E) $\dfrac{1}{2}$

GO ON TO THE NEXT PAGE

39. The measure of the largest angle of the triangle below is

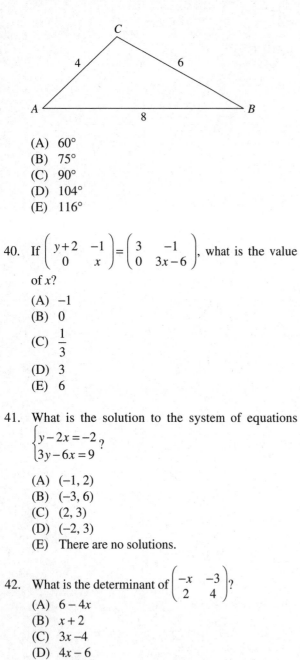

(A) 60°
(B) 75°
(C) 90°
(D) 104°
(E) 116°

40. If $\begin{pmatrix} y+2 & -1 \\ 0 & x \end{pmatrix} = \begin{pmatrix} 3 & -1 \\ 0 & 3x-6 \end{pmatrix}$, what is the value of x?

(A) −1
(B) 0
(C) $\dfrac{1}{3}$
(D) 3
(E) 6

41. What is the solution to the system of equations $\begin{cases} y - 2x = -2 \\ 3y - 6x = 9 \end{cases}$?

(A) (−1, 2)
(B) (−3, 6)
(C) (2, 3)
(D) (−2, 3)
(E) There are no solutions.

42. What is the determinant of $\begin{pmatrix} -x & -3 \\ 2 & 4 \end{pmatrix}$?

(A) $6 - 4x$
(B) $x + 2$
(C) $3x - 4$
(D) $4x - 6$
(E) $-6 - 4x$

GO ON TO THE NEXT PAGE

43. Which point represents $-1 - 2i$?

    (A) A
    (B) B
    (C) C
    (D) D
    (E) E

44. The point $(0, -3, 4)$ lies on the

    (A) xy plane
    (B) xz plane
    (C) yz plane
    (D) x-axis
    (E) z-axis

USE THIS SPACE AS SCRATCH PAPER

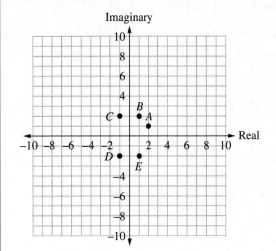

45. The dimensions of a rectangular solid are 4 cm, 6 cm, and 9 cm. The length of the longest segment whose endpoints are vertices of the rectangular solid is

    (A) 3.6 cm
    (B) 4.4 cm
    (C) 8.0 cm
    (D) 11.5 cm
    (E) 14.7 cm

46. If the length, width, and height of a rectangular prism are tripled, the surface area is multiplied by a factor of

    (A) 3
    (B) 6
    (C) 9
    (D) 18
    (E) 27

47. Which of the following shows $(4 + 2i)(6 - 3i)$ in standard form?

    (A) $24i$
    (B) 30
    (C) $10 + i$
    (D) 21
    (E) $24 - 12i$

GO ON TO THE NEXT PAGE

48. $f(x) = mx$ and $g(x) = nx$. If $f(g(x)) = 2x^2 - 1$, what is mn?

(A) $\dfrac{2x-1}{x}$

(B) $2x - \dfrac{1}{x}$

(C) $\dfrac{1}{2} + \dfrac{1}{x}$

(D) $\dfrac{x^2}{2}$

(E) Not enough information

49. Find the area of the triangle below.

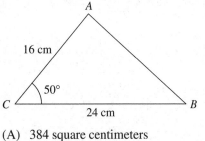

(A) 384 square centimeters
(B) 294 square centimeters
(C) 192 square centimeters
(D) 147 square centimeters
(E) 96 square centimeters

50. Jelly beans come in 5 flavors: orange, cherry, grape, banana, and apple. There are at least 3 of each flavor in the package. Suppose you pick 3 jelly beans at random from the package. How many flavor possibilities are there?

(A) 15
(B) 50
(C) 95
(D) 125
(E) 243

S T O P

IF YOU FINISH BEFORE TIME IS CALLED, YOU MAY CHECK YOUR WORK ON THIS TEST ONLY.
DO NOT TURN TO ANY OTHER TEST IN THIS BOOK.

ANSWER KEY

1. B	11. D	21. B	31. B	41. E
2. C	12. B	22. B	32. D	42. A
3. A	13. D	23. B	33. B	43. D
4. C	14. A	24. C	34. D	44. C
5. C	15. C	25. D	35. B	45. D
6. C	16. D	26. D	36. D	46. C
7. B	17. C	27. E	37. C	47. B
8. D	18. B	28. A	38. E	48. B
9. C	19. A	29. D	39. D	49. D
10. D	20. D	30. D	40. D	50. D

ANSWERS AND EXPLANATIONS

1. **(B)** The radicand cannot be negative. $7 - 2x \geq 0$, so $x \leq 3.5$.

2. **(C)** $f(b)$ directs you to replace x with b, and then simplify. Therefore, $f(b) = 2b^2 + b^2 = 3b^2$.

3. **(A)** Use the equation to find that the center of the circle is at $(2, -1)$ and the radius is 3. Then use the distance formula to find the distance from the center to point $(5, -5)$. $d = \sqrt{(2-5)^2 + (-1-(-5)^2} = 5$. Finally, subtract the radius of the circle from the distance to the given point.

4. **(C)** Rewrite the expression $\log_{\frac{3}{2}} \frac{27}{8}$ as $\left(\frac{3}{2}\right)^x = \frac{27}{8}$, which becomes $\frac{3^x}{2^x} = \frac{27}{8}$. Therefore $x = 3$. Another method is to use the change of base formula and rewrite as $\dfrac{\log\left(\frac{27}{8}\right)}{\log\left(\frac{3}{2}\right)}$ and evaluate on your calculator.

5. **(C)** The vertical asymptotes are nonremovable values of x that make the denominator zero. Set the denominator equal to zero and solve. $x^2 + 3x - 4 = 0$; $(x + 4)(x - 1) = 0$. The factor $(x + 4)$ cancels with the numerator so the only vertical asymptote is $x = 1$. so $x = -4$ and 1.

6. **(C)** Rewrite each equation in the form $y = mx + b$, and then simplify. $x - 2y = 6$ becomes $y = \frac{1}{2}x - 3$.

$ky + 4x = 8$ becomes $y = -\frac{4}{k}x + \frac{8}{k}$. The lines are perpendicular when the slope of one is the negative reciprocal of the other, so k must be 2. Another method is to use using the Standard Form for slope. $Ax + By = C$ where $m = -\left(\frac{A}{B}\right)$. Then you would have $m = -\left(\frac{1}{-2}\right)$ or $\frac{1}{2}$ and $m = -\frac{4}{k}$, therefore k must $= 2$ to make the slope of the perpendicular equation equal to -2.

7. **(B)** The altitude from the vertex to the base bisects both the vertex angle and the base to form two congruent right triangles.

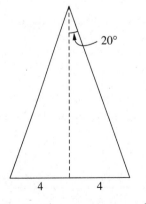

Therefore, $\sin 20° = \dfrac{4}{\text{leg}}$ and $\text{leg} = \dfrac{4}{\sin 20°} = 11.695$. The perimeter equals $11.695 + 11.695 + 8 = 31.39$ cm.

8. **(D)** The x-coordinate is $x = -\dfrac{b}{2a} = -\dfrac{6}{6} = -1$. The y-coordinate is $y = 3(-1)^2 + 6(-1) - 1 = -4$. Therefore, the vertex occurs at the point $(-1, -4)$.

9. **(C)** The line goes through the points $(2, 0)$ and $(6, b)$. Use the formula to find the slope and then use the given slope to solve for b: $m = \dfrac{b-0}{6-2} = \dfrac{b}{4}$ and $\dfrac{b}{4} = \dfrac{1}{2}$, so $b = 2$.

10. **(D)** Use the distance formula to find the radius of the sphere: $d = \sqrt{(1-0)^2 + (3-0)^2 + (5-0)^2} = \sqrt{35}$. Use your calculator to find that $r \approx 5.92$.

11. **(D)** Write the equation in standard form by dividing both sides of the equation by 225 to get $\dfrac{x^2}{9} + \dfrac{y^2}{25} = 1$. Therefore, $a = 5$ and $b = 3$. The length of the major axis equals $2a = 10$.

12. **(B)** $2x^2 - 3x - 2 = (2x + 1)(x - 2) = 0$ when $x = -\dfrac{1}{2}$ or 2. Numbers between these values satisfy the inequality.

13. **(D)** The z-score for A is 0.83, for B is 0.80, for C is 0.75, for D is 1.83, and for E is 0.35.

14. **(A)** One method is to square first to get $4x^{-2}y^4$. Then rewrite as $\dfrac{4y^4}{x^2}$.

15. **(C)** With your calculator in degree mode, enter 2nd tan^{-1}(sin 80°).

16. **(D)** $a_9 = a_1 + [(n-1)d] = 11 + [(9-1)4] = 43$.

17. **(C)** Set your calculator in degree mode. Then find $x = r \cos\theta = 3 \cos 260° = -0.52$ and $y = r \sin\theta = 3 \sin 260° = -2.95$.

18. **(B)** Enter the values into the quadratic formula program on your graphing calculator, or test answers in function. Choose the negative zero and round to the nearest tenth.

19. **(A)** If $x - 2$ is a factor, it should divide into the polynomial without a remainder. Use synthetic division to solve:

2	2	5	k		-16
		4	18		$2k + 36$
	9	$(k + 18)$		$(2k + 20)$

Set the remainder equal to 0 and solve for k: $2k + 20 = 0$, so $k = -10$.

20. **(D)** The probability of both marbles being a color other than blue $= \dfrac{4}{10} \cdot \dfrac{2}{8} = \dfrac{1}{10}$.

21. **(B)** The slope of the given line is -2. The slope of the line that is perpendicular is the negative reciprocal, or $\dfrac{1}{2}$.

22. **(B)** Rewrite the expression using exponents and simplify: $\left(\sqrt[4]{9}\right)^2 = \left(9^{\frac{1}{4}}\right)^2 = 9^{\frac{2}{4}} = 9^{\frac{1}{2}} = \sqrt{9} = 3$.

23. **(B)** Replace $f(x)$ with y. $f(x) = 5x - 2$ becomes $y = 5x - 2$. Then exchange x and y: $x = 5y - 2$. Solve for y: $y = \dfrac{x+2}{5}$.

24. **(C)** One method of solving this problem is by subtracting the equations: $(3x + 2y) - (2x + y) = 8 - 5$, which becomes $x + y = 3$.

25. **(D)** Rewrite the equation for the line in the form $Ax + By + C = 0$: $3x - y + 6 = 0$. Then use the equation $d = \dfrac{|Ax_1 + By_1 + C|}{\sqrt{A^2 + B^2}}$. Therefore, $d = \dfrac{|3(5) + (-1)(2) + 6|}{\sqrt{3^2 + (-1)^2}}$, which simplifies to $\dfrac{19\sqrt{10}}{10}$.

26. **(D)** Rewrite each logarithm to get $a = 3^{\sqrt{2}}$ and $b = 5^{\sqrt{7}}$. Then $ab = 3^{\sqrt{2}} \cdot 5^{\sqrt{7}} \approx 4.7288 \cdot 70.6807 \approx 334$.

27. **(E)** Use the foil method, keeping in mind that one of the terms is itself a binomial. $3x^2(4y + 1) - 3x^2(6xy) - 2xy(4y + 1) + 2xy(6xy)$, which becomes $12x^2y + 3x^2 - 18x^3y - 8xy^2 - 2xy + 12x^2y^2$.

28. **(A)** $(f \cdot g)(x) = f(x) \cdot g(x) = \dfrac{1}{x-4} \cdot \dfrac{1}{x} = \dfrac{1}{x^2 - 4x}$.

29. **(D)** The slope of the line is $\dfrac{5-2}{2-(-4)} = \dfrac{3}{6} = \dfrac{1}{2}$. The point-slope equation is then $y - 5 = \dfrac{1}{2}(x - 2)$. Solve for y to get $y = \dfrac{1}{2}x + 4$. The y-intercept of the line is 4.

30. **(D)** There are 65 data values, so the median is the 33rd largest value, which is 16.

31. **(B)** Find $\dfrac{ab}{ac} = \dfrac{18}{24}$, which becomes $\dfrac{b}{c} = \dfrac{3}{4}$, so $c = \dfrac{4}{3}b$. Substitute this value into the third equation: $bc = 12$ so $b\left(\dfrac{4}{3}b\right) = 12$, which becomes $4b^2 = 36$ and $b = +3$ or -3. The question indicates that the values are positive, so $b = 3$. Therefore, $a = 6$ and $c = 4$, so the sum is $6 + 3 + 4 = 13$.

32. **(D)** First find the measure of angle B: $180 - (70 + 62) = 48°$. Then use the law of sines. $\dfrac{BC}{\sin A} = \dfrac{AC}{\sin B}$, $\dfrac{BC}{\sin 70} = \dfrac{12}{\sin 48}$. Therefore, $BC = \dfrac{12\sin 70}{\sin 48} \approx 15.17$.

33. **(B)** Multiply $22\left(\dfrac{180°}{\pi}\right) = \dfrac{3960°}{\pi}$.

34. **(D)** The total score from the managers must be at least 22.5 (3×7.5). If one manager's score is 7.8, the sum of the remaining scores must be $22.5 - 7.8 = 14.7$. Because the highest the score can be is 8.0, the lowest score the applicant can receive and still be considered in $14.7 - 8.0 = 6.7$.

35. **(B)** Given two sides and the angle between them, use the law of cosines: $c^2 = a^2 + b^2 - 2ab\cdot\cos 105°$. So, $c^2 = 49 + 81 - 2(7)(9)(-0.2588) = 162.6$, and $c = 12.75$. Then use the law of sines: $\dfrac{12.75}{\sin 105} = \dfrac{7}{\sin A}$, $\sin A = \dfrac{7\sin 105}{12.75}$. Therefore, $\angle A$ is 32°.

36. **(D)** Use the change-of-base formula to find $\dfrac{\log 9}{\log 5}$ by entering the values on your calculator.

37. **(C)** There are $\begin{pmatrix}2\\1\end{pmatrix} = 2$ ways of choosing a goalie, $\begin{pmatrix}7\\5\end{pmatrix} = 21$ ways of choosing the defense, and $\begin{pmatrix}8\\5\end{pmatrix} = 56$ ways of choosing the offense. There are $2 \cdot 21 \cdot 56 = 2352$ combinations of players.

38. **(E)** There are four outcomes, two of which are composed of one head and one tail. The probability is therefore $\dfrac{2}{4}$ or $\dfrac{1}{2}$.

39. **(D)** Use the law of cosines, recognizing that the largest angle is $\angle C$ because it is across from the longest side. $c^2 = a^2 + b^2 - 2ab \cdot \cos C$ becomes $64 = 36 + 16 - 2(6)(4)\cos C$, so $\cos C = -0.25$. The measure of $\angle C$ is therefore 104°.

40. **(D)** If the two matrices are equal, $x = 3x - 6$, so $x = 3$.

41. **(E)** Use your graphing calculator to show each equation.

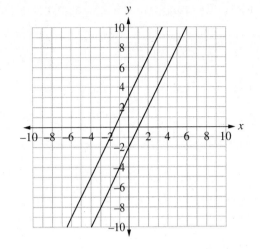

The lines are parallel so they do not intersect at any point.

42. **(A)** The determinant is $ad - bc$, so $-4x - (-6) = -4x + 6$, or $6 - 4x$.

43. **(D)** The horizontal component represents the real part of the number and the vertical component represents the imaginary part. The point that is 1 unit to the left of the origin and 2 units down is D.

44. **(C)** The x-coordinate is zero. Therefore, the point must lie in the yz plane.

45. **(D)** The length of the longest segment is $\sqrt{4^2 + 6^2 + 9^2} = \sqrt{133} \approx 11.5$.

46. **(C)** $SA = 2lw + 2lh + 2wh$. If each dimension is tripled, the surface area becomes: $SA = 2(3l)(3w) + 2(3l)(3h) + 2(3w)(3h) = 9(2lw + 2lh + 2wh)$.

47. **(B)** The fastest method is to enter the problem into your calculator. Use 2nd decimal to enter i. Alternatively, you can use the foil method to multiply and remember to replace i^2 with -1.

48. **(B)** $f(g(x)) = mnx$. Set this equal to $2x^2 - 1$, and solve for mn. $mnx = 2x^2 - 1$; $mnx = x(2x - \dfrac{1}{x})$; $mn = \left(2x - \dfrac{1}{x}\right)$.

49. **(D)** To solve for area, find $A = \dfrac{1}{2}ab \cdot \sin C = \dfrac{1}{2}(24)(16)(0.766) \approx 147$.

50. **(D)** There are 5 possibilities for each jelly bean selected. Therefore, $5^3 = 125$.

▨ DIAGNOSE YOUR STRENGTHS AND WEAKNESSES

Check the number of each question answered correctly and "X" the number of each question answered incorrectly.

Algebra and Functions	1	2	4	5	6	8	9	12	14	18	19	21	Total Number Correct
24 questions													
	22	23	24	25	26	27	28	29	31	36	41	48	

Trigonometry	7	15	32	33	35	39	49	Total Number Correct
7 questions								

Coordinate and Three-Dimensional Geometry	3	10	11	17	44	45	46	Total Number Correct
7 questions								

Numbers and Operations	16	37	40	42	43	47	50	Total Number Correct
7 questions								

Data Analysis, Statistics, and Probability	13	20	30	34	38	Total Number Correct
5 questions						

Number of correct answers $-\dfrac{1}{4}$ **(Number of incorrect answers) = Your raw score**

$$\underline{\hspace{6cm}} - \dfrac{1}{4} \left(\underline{\hspace{5cm}} \right) = \underline{\hspace{4cm}}$$

Compare your raw score with the approximate SAT Subject Test score below:

	Raw Score	SAT Subject Test Approximate Score
Excellent	43–50	770–800
Very Good	33–43	670–770
Good	27–33	620–670
Above Average	21–27	570–620
Average	11–21	500–570
Below Average	< 11	< 500

PRACTICE TEST 5

Treat this practice test as the actual test and complete it in one 60-minute sitting. Use the following answer sheet to fill in your multiple-choice answers. Once you have completed the practice test:

1. Check your answers using the Answer Key.
2. Review the Answers and Solutions.
3. Fill in the "Diagnose Your Strengths and Weaknesses" sheet, and determine areas that require further preparation.

PRACTICE TEST 5

MATH LEVEL 2

Tear out this answer sheet and use it to complete the practice test. Determine the BEST answer for each question. Then, fill in the appropriate oval using a No. 2 pencil.

1. (A)(B)(C)(D)(E)	21. (A)(B)(C)(D)(E)	41. (A)(B)(C)(D)(E)
2. (A)(B)(C)(D)(E)	22. (A)(B)(C)(D)(E)	42. (A)(B)(C)(D)(E)
3. (A)(B)(C)(D)(E)	23. (A)(B)(C)(D)(E)	43. (A)(B)(C)(D)(E)
4. (A)(B)(C)(D)(E)	24. (A)(B)(C)(D)(E)	44. (A)(B)(C)(D)(E)
5. (A)(B)(C)(D)(E)	25. (A)(B)(C)(D)(E)	45. (A)(B)(C)(D)(E)
6. (A)(B)(C)(D)(E)	26. (A)(B)(C)(D)(E)	46. (A)(B)(C)(D)(E)
7. (A)(B)(C)(D)(E)	27. (A)(B)(C)(D)(E)	47. (A)(B)(C)(D)(E)
8. (A)(B)(C)(D)(E)	28. (A)(B)(C)(D)(E)	48. (A)(B)(C)(D)(E)
9. (A)(B)(C)(D)(E)	29. (A)(B)(C)(D)(E)	49. (A)(B)(C)(D)(E)
10. (A)(B)(C)(D)(E)	30. (A)(B)(C)(D)(E)	50. (A)(B)(C)(D)(E)
11. (A)(B)(C)(D)(E)	31. (A)(B)(C)(D)(E)	
12. (A)(B)(C)(D)(E)	32. (A)(B)(C)(D)(E)	
13. (A)(B)(C)(D)(E)	33. (A)(B)(C)(D)(E)	
14. (A)(B)(C)(D)(E)	34. (A)(B)(C)(D)(E)	
15. (A)(B)(C)(D)(E)	35. (A)(B)(C)(D)(E)	
16. (A)(B)(C)(D)(E)	36. (A)(B)(C)(D)(E)	
17. (A)(B)(C)(D)(E)	37. (A)(B)(C)(D)(E)	
18. (A)(B)(C)(D)(E)	38. (A)(B)(C)(D)(E)	
19. (A)(B)(C)(D)(E)	39. (A)(B)(C)(D)(E)	
20. (A)(B)(C)(D)(E)	40. (A)(B)(C)(D)(E)	

PRACTICE TEST 5

Time: 60 minutes

Directions: Select the BEST answer for each of the 50 multiple-choice questions. If the exact solution is not one of the five choices, select the answer that is the best approximation. Then, fill in the appropriate oval on the answer sheet.

Notes:

1. A calculator will be needed to answer some of the questions on the test. Scientific, programmable, and graphing calculators are permitted. It is up to you to determine when and when not to use your calculator.
2. Angles on the Level 2 test are measured in degrees and radians. You need to decide whether your calculator should be set to degree mode or radian mode for a particular question.
3. Figures are drawn as accurately as possible and are intended to help solve some of the test problems. If a figure is not drawn to scale, this will be stated in the problem. All figures lie in a plane unless the problem indicates otherwise.
4. Unless otherwise stated, the domain of a function f is assumed to be the set of real numbers x for which the value of the function, $f(x)$, is a real number.
5. Reference information that may be useful in answering some of the test questions can be found below.

Reference Information
Right circular cone with radius r and height h: Volume $= \dfrac{1}{3}\pi r^2 h$
Right circular cone with circumference of base c and slant height ℓ: Lateral Area $= \dfrac{1}{2}c\ell$
Sphere with radius r: Volume $= \dfrac{4}{3}\pi r^3$ Surface Area $= 4\pi r^2$
Pyramid with base area B and height h: Volume $= \dfrac{1}{3}Bh$

▬ PRACTICE TEST 5 QUESTIONS

1. The 10th term of an arithmetic sequence with a common difference of 6 is 62. What is the first term of the sequence?

   (A) 6
   (B) 8
   (C) 10
   (D) 12
   (E) 14

2. Find the area of the triangle below.

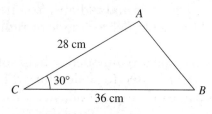

   (A) 189 square centimeters
   (B) 252 square centimeters
   (C) 192 square centimeters
   (D) 504 square centimeters
   (E) 1008 square centimeters

3. What is the distance between points $P(2, 1, 0)$ and $R(-1, 2, 3)$?

   (A) 3.2
   (B) 4.4
   (C) 4.6
   (D) 5.1
   (E) 5.8

4. What is the difference, to the nearest whole number, between the lateral area of the cylinder below and the sum of the areas of the two bases?

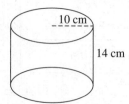

   (A) 80 square centimeters
   (B) 100 square centimeters
   (C) 157 square centimeters
   (D) 251 square centimeters
   (E) 314 square centimeters

GO ON TO THE NEXT PAGE

5. The measure of the largest angle of the triangle below is

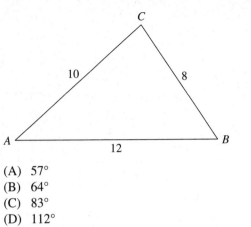

(A) 57°
(B) 64°
(C) 83°
(D) 112°
(E) 125°

6. There are 14 girls and 12 boys at a party. If 3 party guests are selected at random, what is the probability that they will all be girls?

(A) $\dfrac{3}{14}$

(B) $\dfrac{7}{50}$

(C) $\dfrac{3}{26}$

(D) $\dfrac{7}{26}$

(E) $\dfrac{2}{3}$

7. If a, b, and c are positive, with $ab = 4$, $ac = 3$, and $bc = 12$, then $a + b + c =$

(A) 8
(B) 12
(C) 16
(D) 22
(E) 48

8. If the range of a set of integers is 5 and the mean is 35, which of the following statements must be true?

    I. The mode is 35.
    II. The median is 35.
    III. There are exactly 5 data values.

(A) I only
(B) II and III
(C) I and III
(D) I, II, and III
(E) None of the statements must be true.

GO ON TO THE NEXT PAGE

USE THIS SPACE AS SCRATCH PAPER

9. If $f(x) = 2x^2 + 3x - 2$, then $f(2a) =$

(A) $2(a^2 + a)$

(B) $2a^2 + 3a - 2$

(C) $8a^2 - 2$

(D) $4a^2 + 3a - 1$

(E) $2(4a^2 + 3a - 1)$

10. If $\log_x 16 = 2$, and $\log_x 64 = y$, what is the value of y?

(A) 3

(B) 6

(C) 8

(D) 16

(E) 64

11. Which point lies inside the circle described by the equation $(x - 2)^2 + (y + 4)^2 = 9$?

(A) $(1, -2)$

(B) $(5, -5)$

(C) $(0, -8)$

(D) $(3, 0)$

(E) $(-2, -3)$

12. The slope of the linear function, f, is -2. If $f(1) = 1$ and $f(4) = n$, what is n?

(A) -6

(B) -5

(C) -3

(D) $\dfrac{1}{2}$

(E) 4

13. What is the length of the major axis of the ellipse whose equation is $9x^2 + 4y^2 = 36$?

(A) 3

(B) 4

(C) 6

(D) 9

(E) 13

14. What is the distance from point $(2, -2)$ to line $3x + 4y = 2$?

(A) 1.9

(B) 1.6

(C) 1.1

(D) 0.8

(E) 0.4

15. If $x + 2$ is a factor of $x^3 + 4x^2 + kx + 10$, what is the value of k?

(A) -10

(B) -7

(C) 1

(D) 9

(E) 18

GO ON TO THE NEXT PAGE

16. If $3x + 2y = 9$ and $2x + 3y = 11$, what is $x - y$?

    (A) -2
    (B) -1
    (C) 0
    (D) 2
    (E) 3

17. What are the coordinates of the vertex of the parabola whose equation is $y = 2x^2 + 8x - 4$?

    (A) $(-1, 4)$
    (B) $(-1, -2)$
    (C) $(1, 6)$
    (D) $(12, 4)$
    (E) $(-2, -12)$

18. The y-intercept of the line that passes through the points $(-2, 9)$ and $(4, 0)$ is

    (A) -3
    (B) $-\dfrac{1}{2}$
    (C) $\dfrac{3}{2}$
    (D) 6
    (E) 9

19. The vertex angle of an isosceles triangle is $32°$. If the length of the base is 12 centimeters, what is the perimeter of the triangle?

    (A) 12.83 cm
    (B) 33.77 cm
    (C) 43.54 cm
    (D) 55.54 cm
    (E) 65.30 cm

20. What is the radius of a sphere with the center at the origin that passes through the point $(-2, -1, 1)$?

    (A) 1.41
    (B) 2
    (C) 2.45
    (D) 3
    (E) 6

21. If $\log_2 m = 8$ and $\log_5 n = 4$, $mn =$

    (A) 3906
    (B) 4096
    (C) $25,600$
    (D) $160,000$
    (E) $625,000$

USE THIS SPACE AS SCRATCH PAPER

GO ON TO THE NEXT PAGE

22. What is the solution to the system of equations
$\begin{cases} x+y=4 \\ 2x-3y=-2 \end{cases}$?

    (A) $(-2, 2)$
    (B) $(-2, 0)$
    (C) $(2, 2)$
    (D) $(2, -4)$
    (E) There are no solutions.

23. $f(x) = mx$ and $g(x) = nx$. If $f(g(x)) = 3x^2 + 2$, what is mn?

    (A) $\dfrac{3x-2}{x}$

    (B) $\dfrac{x^2}{3}$

    (C) $3x + \dfrac{2}{x}$

    (D) $3x - \dfrac{1}{x}$

    (E) Not enough information is given.

24. A craft store sells 6 colors of beads: white, blue, red, green, clear, and black. Suppose you pick 4 beads from a large bin at random. If there are at least 4 beads of every color, how many color possibilities are there?

    (A) 24
    (B) 466
    (C) 640
    (D) 1296
    (E) 4096

25. Which of the following lines are vertical asymptotes of the graph of $y = \dfrac{x^2 + 2x + 4}{x^2 - x - 6}$?

    I. $x = -2$
    II. $x = 0$
    III. $x = 3$

    (A) I only
    (B) II only
    (C) III only
    (D) I and III
    (E) II and III

USE THIS SPACE AS SCRATCH PAPER

GO ON TO THE NEXT PAGE

26. $\dfrac{2}{\sqrt[3]{2}} =$

    (A) $\sqrt{3}$

    (B) $\dfrac{\sqrt{3}}{\sqrt{2}}$

    (C) $\dfrac{1}{\sqrt{3}}$

    (D) $\sqrt{2}$

    (E) $\sqrt[3]{4}$

27. Which of the following is perpendicular to the line $y = \dfrac{2}{3}x - 1$?

    (A) $y = -\dfrac{3}{2}x + 4$

    (B) $y = \dfrac{3}{2}x + 1$

    (C) $y = x + \dfrac{3}{2}$

    (D) $y = -2x + 4$

    (E) $y = 2x - 4$

28. If $f(x) = \sqrt{x-6}$, then $f^{-1}(x)$ is

    (A) $\dfrac{1}{x^2 + 6}$

    (B) $x^2 - 6$

    (C) $\dfrac{x^2}{6}$

    (D) $x^2 + 6$

    (E) $x + 36$

29. Which of the following is a solution to $3x^2 + x < 2$?

    (A) $-\dfrac{2}{3} < x < 1$

    (B) $-2 < x < 3$

    (C) $-1 < x < \dfrac{2}{3}$

    (D) $-1 < x$

    (E) $x < -1$ or $x > \dfrac{2}{3}$

GO ON TO THE NEXT PAGE

30. How can $\dfrac{a^{-1}b}{a^{-1}+b^{-1}}$ be expressed with only positive exponents?

    (A) $\dfrac{a^2+b^2}{b^2}$

    (B) $\dfrac{a+b}{b^2}$

    (C) $\dfrac{b^2}{2ab}$

    (D) $\dfrac{b^2}{b+a}$

    (E) $\dfrac{b^2}{ab+a^2}$

31. $(2x^2 - 3xy)((3y + 4) - xy) =$
    (A) $6x^2y + 8x^2 - 2x^3y$
    (B) $-12xy + 3x^2y^2$
    (C) $x^3y + 12x^2y^2$
    (D) $-1x^2y + 3x^2 - 12x^3y - xy^2$
    (E) $6x^2y + 8x^2 - 2x^3y - 9xy^2 - 12xy + 3x^2y^2$

32. The ages of people at a family reunion are given below. What is the mean age?

41
21
28
68
86
32
28
36
42
50
56
64

    (A) 28
    (B) 46
    (C) 54
    (D) 65
    (E) 86

33. $240°$ is equivalent to

    (A) $\dfrac{\pi^R}{2}$

    (B) $\dfrac{4\pi^R}{3}$

    (C) $3\pi^R$

    (D) $\dfrac{3\pi^R}{4}$

    (E) $\dfrac{24\pi^R}{3}$

GO ON TO THE NEXT PAGE ▶

34. $\begin{pmatrix} 1 & -1 & 0 \\ 2 & 3 & -2 \end{pmatrix} + \begin{pmatrix} 2 & -2 & 6 \\ 4 & 1 & -3 \end{pmatrix} =$

(A) $\begin{pmatrix} 1 & -2 & 3 \\ 2 & 2 & 1 \end{pmatrix}$

(B) $\begin{pmatrix} 3 & -3 & 6 \\ 6 & 4 & -5 \end{pmatrix}$

(C) $\begin{pmatrix} -3 & -3 & -6 \\ -2 & 2 & -5 \end{pmatrix}$

(D) $\begin{pmatrix} 4 & 0 & -3 \\ 3 & 1 & 2 \end{pmatrix}$

(E) $\begin{pmatrix} 2 & 2 & 0 \\ 8 & 3 & 6 \end{pmatrix}$

35. What is the measure of *BC* in the triangle below?

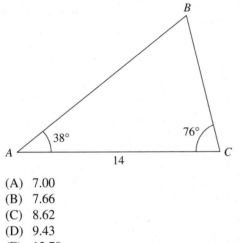

(A) 7.00
(B) 7.66
(C) 8.62
(D) 9.43
(E) 12.79

36. A player in a game rolls the number cube and spins the spinner. What is the probability that the player will roll an even number on the number cube and spin an even number on the spinner?

(A) $\dfrac{1}{12}$

(B) $\dfrac{1}{8}$

(C) $\dfrac{1}{6}$

(D) $\dfrac{1}{4}$

(E) $\dfrac{1}{2}$

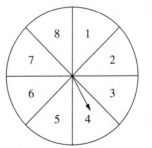

GO ON TO THE NEXT PAGE

37. To the nearest tenth, the positive zero of $y = 3x^2 + 2x - 4$ is

    (A) 0.5
    (B) 0.6
    (C) 0.9
    (D) 1.2
    (E) 1.5

38. If $f(x) = \dfrac{1}{x-4}$ and $g(x) = \dfrac{1}{x}$, $\left(\dfrac{f}{g}\right)(x)$ equals

    (A) $\dfrac{1}{x^2 - 4x}$

    (B) $\dfrac{2x}{x-4}$

    (C) $\dfrac{2x-4}{x^2 - 4x}$

    (D) $\dfrac{x}{x-4}$

    (E) $x + \dfrac{1}{4}$

39. Samantha is choosing 3 side dishes to go with her meal. She has 12 side dishes to choose from. How many different combinations can Samantha choose?

    (A) 36
    (B) 108
    (C) 220
    (D) 324
    (E) 600

40. Evaluate $\sin^{-1}(\sin 100°)$.

    (A) 10
    (B) 56
    (C) 68
    (D) 80
    (E) 92

41. Which point represents $-3 + 4i$?

    (A) A
    (B) B
    (C) C
    (D) D
    (E) E

USE THIS SPACE AS SCRATCH PAPER

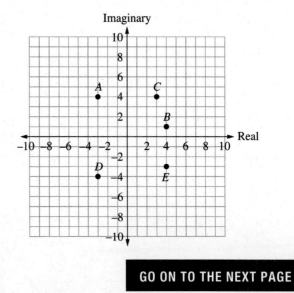

GO ON TO THE NEXT PAGE

42. What is the distance between point $P(4, -1, 3)$ and the origin?

    (A) 2.2
    (B) 3.3
    (C) 5.1
    (D) 5.4
    (E) 6.0

43. What is the determinant of $\begin{pmatrix} -2 & 4 \\ p+1 & 1 \end{pmatrix}$?

    (A) $6 - 4p$
    (B) $-6 - 4p$
    (C) $4p - 4$
    (D) $4p - 6$
    (E) $-2 - 4p$

44. A sphere with diameter 6 inches is inscribed in a cube. What is the volume of the space between the sphere and the cube?

    (A) 96 in.^3
    (B) 103 in.^3
    (C) 113 in.^3
    (D) 126 in.^3
    (E) 216 in.^3

45. The polar coordinates of point P are $(4, 160°)$. The rectangular coordinates of point P are

    (A) $(-3.76, 1.37)$
    (B) $(-0.94, 0.34)$
    (C) $(0.99, 0.69)$
    (D) $(-2.35, 8.56)$
    (E) $(-0.36, -1.46)$

46. $\log_6 8 =$

    (A) 0.70
    (B) 0.90
    (C) 1.08
    (D) 1.16
    (E) 1.21

47. What is the domain of $f(x) = \dfrac{x+6}{x^2 - 4}$?

    (A) $\{x: x \neq -1 \text{ and } x \neq 1\}$
    (B) $\{x: x \neq 0\}$
    (C) $\{x: x \neq -4 \text{ and } x \neq 4\}$
    (D) $\{x: x \neq -2 \text{ and } x \neq 2\}$
    (E) all real numbers

GO ON TO THE NEXT PAGE

48. What are the odds of rolling a number greater than 4 when one die is thrown?

(A) $\dfrac{1}{4}$

(B) $\dfrac{1}{3}$

(C) $\dfrac{1}{2}$

(D) $\dfrac{2}{3}$

(E) $\dfrac{3}{4}$

49. What is the measure of $\angle A$ in the triangle below?

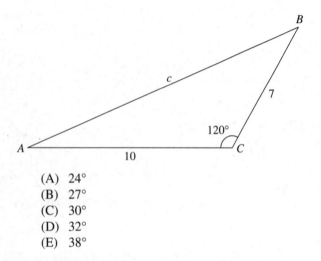

(A) 24°
(B) 27°
(C) 30°
(D) 32°
(E) 38°

50. Which of the following shows $(4 - 2i)(3 + 2i)$ in standard form?

(A) $4i$
(B) $12 - 2i$
(C) $16 + 2i$
(D) 12
(E) $14 - 12i$

S T O P

IF YOU FINISH BEFORE TIME IS CALLED, YOU MAY CHECK YOUR WORK ON THIS TEST ONLY.
DO NOT TURN TO ANY OTHER TEST IN THIS BOOK.

ANSWER KEY

1. B	11. A	21. D	31. E	41. A
2. B	12. B	22. C	32. B	42. C
3. B	13. C	23. C	33. B	43. B
4. D	14. D	24. D	34. B	44. B
5. C	15. D	25. C	35. D	45. A
6. B	16. A	26. E	36. D	46. D
7. A	17. E	27. A	37. C	47. D
8. E	18. D	28. D	38. D	48. C
9. E	19. D	29. C	39. C	49. A
10. A	20. C	30. D	40. D	50. C

ANSWERS AND EXPLANATIONS

1. **(B)** $a_n = a_1 + [(n-1)d]$: $62 = a + [(10-1)6]$. Solve for $a = 8$.

2. **(B)** To solve for area, find $A = \frac{1}{2}ab \cdot \sin C = \frac{1}{2}(36)(28)(0.5) = 252$.

3. **(B)** Use the distance formula in three dimensions: $d = \sqrt{(2-(-1)^2 + (1-2)^2 + (0-3)^2} = \sqrt{9+1+9} \approx 4.4$.

4. **(D)** The lateral area is $2\pi rh = 280\pi$. The area of each base is $\pi r^2 = 100\pi$. The difference is $280\pi - 2(100\pi) = 80\pi$, which is about 251.2.

5. **(C)** Use the law of cosines, recognizing that the largest angle is $\angle C$ because it is across from the longest side. $c^2 = a^2 + b^2 - 2ab \cdot \cos C$ becomes $144 = 64 + 100 - 2(8)(10)\cos C$, so $\cos C = 0.125$. The measure of $\angle C$ is therefore 83°.

6. **(B)** The probability that the first guest chosen is a girl is $\frac{14}{26}$, or $\frac{7}{13}$. That leaves 13 girls, so the probability that the next guest chosen is a girl is $\frac{13}{25}$ and the probability that the third guest chosen is a girl is $\frac{12}{24}$, or $\frac{1}{2}$. The probability that all three guests are girls is $\frac{7}{13} \cdot \frac{13}{25} \cdot \frac{1}{2} = \frac{7}{50}$.

7. **(A)** Find $\frac{ab}{ac} = \frac{4}{3}$, which becomes $\frac{b}{c} = \frac{3}{4}$, so $c = \frac{3}{4}b$. Substitute this value into the third equation: $bc = 12$, so $b\left(\frac{3}{4}\right)b = 12$, which becomes $3b^2 = 48$ and $b = 4$. Therefore, $a = 1$ and $c = 3$, so the sum is $1 + 4 + 3 = 8$.

8. **(E)** The data values could have a mean of 35 without 35 being one of the values, so I is not always true. The median is the middle data value, and is not necessarily the same as the mean so II is not always true. There can be any number of data values as long as they average to 35 and stay within a range of 5. Therefore, III is not always true.

9. **(E)** $f(2a)$ directs you to replace x with $2a$, and then simplify. Therefore, $f(2a) = 2(2a)^2 + 3(2a) - 2 = 8a^2 + 6a - 2 = 2(4a^2 + 3a - 1)$.

10. **(A)** Rewrite the first logarithm to solve for x: $\log_x 16 = 2$ as $x^2 = 16$, so $x = 4$. Then substitute the value of x into the second logarithm to solve for y: write $\log_4 64$ as $4^y = 64$, so $y = 3$.

11. **(A)** The center of the circle is at $(2, -4)$ and the radius is 3. Either enter the equation into your calculator and analyze each point from a graph, or use the distance formula to find the distance between each point and the center. If the distance is greater than the radius, the point is outside the circle. For (A), $d = \sqrt{(1-2)^2 + (-2-(-4))^2} = \sqrt{5} \approx 2.2$. Therefore, this point lies inside the circle.

12. **(B)** The line goes through the points $(1, 1)$ and $(4, n)$. Use the formula to find the slope and then use the given slope to solve for b: $m = \dfrac{n-1}{4-1} = \dfrac{n-1}{3}$ and $\dfrac{n-1}{3} = -2$, so $n = -5$.

13. **(C)** Write the equation in standard form by dividing both sides of the equation by 36 to get $\dfrac{x^2}{4} + \dfrac{y^2}{9} = 1$. Therefore, $a = 3$ and $b = 2$. The length of the major axis equals $2a = 6$.

14. **(D)** Rewrite the equation for the line in the form $Ax + By + C = 0$: $3x + 4y - 2 = 0$. Then use the equation $d = \dfrac{|Ax_1 + By_1 + C|}{\sqrt{A^2 + B^2}}$. Therefore, $d = \dfrac{|3(2) + (4)(-2) + (-2)|}{\sqrt{3^2 + 4^2}}$, which simplifies to $\dfrac{4}{5}$, or 0.8.

15. **(D)** If $x + 2$ is a factor, it should divide into the polynomial without a remainder. Use synthetic division to solve:

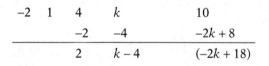

-2	1	4	k	10
		-2	-4	$-2k + 8$
	2	$k - 4$	$(-2k + 18)$

Set the remainder equal to 0 and solve for k: $-2k + 18 = 0$, so $k = 9$.

16. **(A)** One method to solve this problem is to subtract the equations: $(3x + 2y) - (2x + 3y) = 9 - 11$, which becomes $x - y = -2$.

17. **(E)** The x-coordinate is $x = -\dfrac{b}{2a} = -\dfrac{8}{4} = -2$. The y-coordinate is $y = 2(-2)^2 + 8(-2) - 4 = -12$. Therefore, the vertex occurs at the point $(-2, -12)$.

18. **(D)** The slope of the line is $\dfrac{9-0}{-2-4} = \dfrac{9}{-6} = -\dfrac{3}{2}$. The point-slope equation is then $y - 9 = -\dfrac{3}{2}(x + 2)$. Solve for y to get $y = -\dfrac{3}{2}x + 6$. The y-intercept of the line is 6.

19. **(D)** The altitude from the vertex to the base bisects both the vertex angle and the base to form two congruent right triangles.

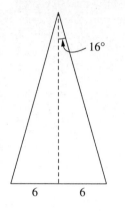

Therefore, $\sin 16° = \dfrac{6}{\text{leg}}$ and $\text{leg} = \dfrac{6}{\sin 16°} = 21.768$. The perimeter equals $21.768 + 21.768 + 12 = 55.54$ cm.

20. **(C)** Use the distance formula to find the radius of the sphere: $d = \sqrt{(-2-0)^2 + (-1-0)^2 + (1-0)^2} = \sqrt{6}$. Use your calculator to find that $r \approx 2.45$.

21. **(D)** Rewrite each logarithm to get $m = 2^8$ and $n = 5^4$. Then $mn = 256 \cdot 625 = 160{,}000$.

22. **(C)** Rewrite the equations in slope-intercept form and then use your graphing calculator to show each equation.

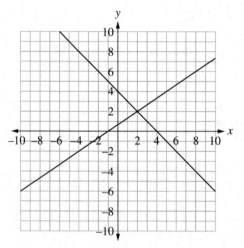

The lines intersect at $(2, 2)$. Alternate methods include substitution and elimination.

23. **(C)** $f(g(x)) = mnx$. Set this equal to $3x^2 + 2$, and solve for mn. $mnx = 3x^2 + 2$; $mn = \dfrac{3x^2}{x} + \dfrac{2}{x}$; $mn = \left(3x + \dfrac{2}{x}\right)$.

24. **(D)** There are 6 possibilities for each bead selected. Therefore, $6^4 = 1296$.

25. **(C)** The vertical asymptotes are the nonremovable values of x that make the denominator zero. Set the denominator equal to zero and $(x + 2)$ cancels with the numerator, so the only vertical asymptote is $x = 3$. Solve $x^2 - x - 6 = 0$; $(x + 2)(x - 3) = 0$.

26. **(E)** Simplify by using rational exponents: $\dfrac{2}{\sqrt[3]{2}} = \dfrac{2}{2^{\frac{1}{3}}} = 2^{1-\frac{1}{3}} = 2^{\frac{2}{3}} = \sqrt[3]{2^2} = \sqrt[3]{4}$.

27. **(A)** The slope of the given line is $\dfrac{2}{3}$. The slope of the line that is perpendicular is the negative reciprocal, or $-\dfrac{3}{2}$.

28. **(D)** Replace $f(x)$ with y. $f(x) = \sqrt{x-6}$ becomes $y = \sqrt{x-6}$. Then switch x with y: $x = \sqrt{y-6}$. Solve for y: $x^2 = y - 6$ so $y = x^2 + 6$.

29. **(C)** $3x^2 + x - 2 = (3x - 2)(x + 1) = 0$ when $x = \dfrac{2}{3}$ or -1. Numbers between these values satisfy the inequality.

30. **(D)** Rewrite as $\dfrac{\frac{b}{a}}{\frac{1}{a} + \frac{1}{b}}$, and then rewrite the denominator with a common denominator: $\dfrac{\frac{b}{a}}{\frac{b+a}{ab}}$ multiply: $\dfrac{\frac{b}{a}}{\frac{b+a}{ab}} = \dfrac{b}{a} \cdot \dfrac{ab}{b+a} = \dfrac{ab^2}{ab + a^2} = \dfrac{b^2}{b+a}$.

31. **(E)** Use the foil method, keeping in mind that one of the terms is itself a binomial. $2x^2(3y + 4) - 2x^2(xy) - 3xy(3y + 4) + 3xy(xy)$, which becomes $6x^2y + 8x^2 - 2x^3y - 9xy^2 - 12xy + 3x^2y^2$.

32. **(B)** Add the ages to get a sum of 552, and then divide by the number of data values, which is 12.

33. **(B)** To get radians, multiply by $\left(\dfrac{\pi}{180°}\right)$. So $240° \left(\dfrac{\pi}{180°}\right) = \dfrac{240\pi}{180°} = \dfrac{4\pi^R}{3}$.

34. **(B)** Add the corresponding elements of each matrix. $\begin{pmatrix} 1 & -1 & 0 \\ 2 & 3 & -2 \end{pmatrix} + \begin{pmatrix} 2 & -2 & 6 \\ 4 & 1 & -3 \end{pmatrix} = \begin{pmatrix} 3 & -3 & 6 \\ 6 & 4 & -5 \end{pmatrix}$

35. **(D)** First find the measure of angle B: $180 - (76 + 38) = 66°$. Then use the law of sines. $\dfrac{BC}{\sin A} = \dfrac{AC}{\sin B}$, $\dfrac{BC}{\sin 38} = \dfrac{14}{\sin 66}$. Therefore, $BC = \dfrac{14 \sin 38}{\sin 66} \approx 9.43$.

36. **(D)** The probability of rolling an even number $= \dfrac{3}{6} = \dfrac{1}{2}$. The probability of spinning an even number $= \dfrac{4}{8} = \dfrac{1}{2}$. The probability of rolling an even number and spinning an even number $= \dfrac{1}{2} \cdot \dfrac{1}{2} = \dfrac{1}{4}$.

37. **(C)** Enter the values into the quadratic formula program on your graphing calculator, or test answers in function. Choose the positive zero and round to the nearest tenth.

38. **(D)** $\left(\dfrac{f}{g}\right) x = \dfrac{f(x)}{g(x)} = \dfrac{1}{x-4} \div \dfrac{1}{x} = \dfrac{1}{x-4} \cdot x = \dfrac{x}{x-4}$.

39. **(C)** Enter 12 MATH/PRB/nCr 3 into your calculator to solve or solve as $\dfrac{12!}{(12-3)!3!} = 220$.

40. **(D)** With your calculator in degree mode, enter 2nd $\sin^{-1}(\sin 100°)$.

41. **(A)** The horizontal component represents the real part of the number and the vertical component represents the imaginary part. The point that is 3 units to the left of the origin and 4 units up is A.

42. **(C)** Use the distance formula in three dimensions: $d = \sqrt{(4-0)^2 + (-1-0)^2 + (3-0)^2} = \sqrt{16 + 1 + 9} \approx 5.1$.

43. **(B)** The determinant is $ad - bc$, so $-2 - [4(p + 1)] = -2 - (4p + 4) = -2 - 4p - 4 = -6 - 4p$.

44. **(B)** The radius of the sphere is 3 inches. Find the volume of the sphere: $V = \dfrac{4}{3}\pi(3)^3 \approx 113$. The length of each side of the cube is 6 inches. Find the volume of the cube: $V = 6^3 = 216$. The difference is: $216 - 113 = 103$ in.^{3}

45. **(A)** Set your calculator in degree mode. Then find $x = r \cos \theta = 4 \cos 160° = -3.76$ and $y = r \sin \theta = 4 \sin 160° = 1.37$.

46. **(D)** Use the change-of-base formula to find $\dfrac{\log 8}{\log 6}$ by entering the values on your calculator.

47. **(D)** Determine the values of x that would make the denominator 0. Factor the denominator to $(x - 2)(x + 2) = 0$, and then solve to find that $x = -2$ or 2.

48. **(C)** The odds of an event happening is defined as the probability of the event happening divided by the probability of the event not happening. The probability of the event happening is $\frac{2}{6}$, or $\frac{1}{3}$. The probability of the event not happening is $\frac{4}{6}$, or $\frac{2}{3}$. Therefore, the odds $= \dfrac{\frac{1}{3}}{\frac{2}{3}} = \frac{1}{2}$.

49. **(A)** Given two sides and the angle between them, use the law of cosines: $c^2 = a^2 + b^2 - 2ab \cdot \cos 120°$. So, $c^2 = 49 + 100 - 2(7)(10)(-0.5) = 219$, and $c = 14.8$. Then use the law of sines: $\dfrac{14.8}{\sin 120} = \dfrac{7}{\sin A}$, $\sin A = \dfrac{7 \sin 120}{14.8}$. Therefore, $\angle A$ is 24°.

50. **(C)** The fastest method is to enter the problem into your calculator. Use 2nd decimal to enter i. Alternatively, you can use the foil method to multiply and remember to replace i^2 with -1. $(4 - 2i)(3 + 2i) = 12 + 8i - 6i - 4i^2 = 12 + 2i + 4 = 16 + 2i$.

▓▓▓ DIAGNOSE YOUR STRENGTHS AND WEAKNESSES

Check the number of each question answered correctly and "X" the number of each question answered incorrectly.

Algebra and Functions	7	9	10	12	14	15	16	17	18	21	22	23	Total Number Correct
23 questions													
	25	26	27	28	29	30	31	37	38	46	47		

Trigonometry	2	5	19	33	35	40	49	Total Number Correct
7 questions								

Coordinate and Three-Dimensional Geometry	3	4	11	13	20	42	44	45	Total Number Correct
8 questions									

Numbers and Operations	1	24	34	39	41	43	50	Total Number Correct
7 questions								

Data Analysis, Statistics, and Probability	6	8	32	36	48	Total Number Correct
5 questions						

Number of correct answers $-\dfrac{1}{4}$ **(Number of incorrect answers) = Your raw score**

_____ $-\dfrac{1}{4}$ (_____) = _____

Compare your raw score with the approximate SAT Subject Test score below:

	Raw Score	SAT Subject Test Approximate Score
Excellent	43–50	770–800
Very Good	33–43	670–770
Good	27–33	620–670
Above Average	21–27	570–620
Average	11–21	500–570
Below Average	< 11	< 500

PRACTICE TEST 6

Treat this practice test as the actual test and complete it in one 60-minute sitting. Use the following answer sheet to fill in your multiple-choice answers. Once you have completed the practice test:

1. Check your answers using the Answer Key.
2. Review the Answers and Solutions.
3. Fill in the "Diagnose Your Strengths and Weaknesses" sheet, and determine areas that require further preparation.

PRACTICE TEST 6

MATH LEVEL 2

ANSWER SHEET

Tear out this answer sheet and use it to complete the practice test. Determine the BEST answer for each question. Then, fill in the appropriate oval using a No. 2 pencil.

1. Ⓐ Ⓑ Ⓒ Ⓓ Ⓔ	21. Ⓐ Ⓑ Ⓒ Ⓓ Ⓔ	41. Ⓐ Ⓑ Ⓒ Ⓓ Ⓔ
2. Ⓐ Ⓑ Ⓒ Ⓓ Ⓔ	22. Ⓐ Ⓑ Ⓒ Ⓓ Ⓔ	42. Ⓐ Ⓑ Ⓒ Ⓓ Ⓔ
3. Ⓐ Ⓑ Ⓒ Ⓓ Ⓔ	23. Ⓐ Ⓑ Ⓒ Ⓓ Ⓔ	43. Ⓐ Ⓑ Ⓒ Ⓓ Ⓔ
4. Ⓐ Ⓑ Ⓒ Ⓓ Ⓔ	24. Ⓐ Ⓑ Ⓒ Ⓓ Ⓔ	44. Ⓐ Ⓑ Ⓒ Ⓓ Ⓔ
5. Ⓐ Ⓑ Ⓒ Ⓓ Ⓔ	25. Ⓐ Ⓑ Ⓒ Ⓓ Ⓔ	45. Ⓐ Ⓑ Ⓒ Ⓓ Ⓔ
6. Ⓐ Ⓑ Ⓒ Ⓓ Ⓔ	26. Ⓐ Ⓑ Ⓒ Ⓓ Ⓔ	46. Ⓐ Ⓑ Ⓒ Ⓓ Ⓔ
7. Ⓐ Ⓑ Ⓒ Ⓓ Ⓔ	27. Ⓐ Ⓑ Ⓒ Ⓓ Ⓔ	47. Ⓐ Ⓑ Ⓒ Ⓓ Ⓔ
8. Ⓐ Ⓑ Ⓒ Ⓓ Ⓔ	28. Ⓐ Ⓑ Ⓒ Ⓓ Ⓔ	48. Ⓐ Ⓑ Ⓒ Ⓓ Ⓔ
9. Ⓐ Ⓑ Ⓒ Ⓓ Ⓔ	29. Ⓐ Ⓑ Ⓒ Ⓓ Ⓔ	49. Ⓐ Ⓑ Ⓒ Ⓓ Ⓔ
10. Ⓐ Ⓑ Ⓒ Ⓓ Ⓔ	30. Ⓐ Ⓑ Ⓒ Ⓓ Ⓔ	50. Ⓐ Ⓑ Ⓒ Ⓓ Ⓔ
11. Ⓐ Ⓑ Ⓒ Ⓓ Ⓔ	31. Ⓐ Ⓑ Ⓒ Ⓓ Ⓔ	
12. Ⓐ Ⓑ Ⓒ Ⓓ Ⓔ	32. Ⓐ Ⓑ Ⓒ Ⓓ Ⓔ	
13. Ⓐ Ⓑ Ⓒ Ⓓ Ⓔ	33. Ⓐ Ⓑ Ⓒ Ⓓ Ⓔ	
14. Ⓐ Ⓑ Ⓒ Ⓓ Ⓔ	34. Ⓐ Ⓑ Ⓒ Ⓓ Ⓔ	
15. Ⓐ Ⓑ Ⓒ Ⓓ Ⓔ	35. Ⓐ Ⓑ Ⓒ Ⓓ Ⓔ	
16. Ⓐ Ⓑ Ⓒ Ⓓ Ⓔ	36. Ⓐ Ⓑ Ⓒ Ⓓ Ⓔ	
17. Ⓐ Ⓑ Ⓒ Ⓓ Ⓔ	37. Ⓐ Ⓑ Ⓒ Ⓓ Ⓔ	
18. Ⓐ Ⓑ Ⓒ Ⓓ Ⓔ	38. Ⓐ Ⓑ Ⓒ Ⓓ Ⓔ	
19. Ⓐ Ⓑ Ⓒ Ⓓ Ⓔ	39. Ⓐ Ⓑ Ⓒ Ⓓ Ⓔ	
20. Ⓐ Ⓑ Ⓒ Ⓓ Ⓔ	40. Ⓐ Ⓑ Ⓒ Ⓓ Ⓔ	

PRACTICE TEST 6

Time: 60 minutes

Directions: Select the BEST answer for each of the 50 multiple-choice questions. If the exact solution is not one of the five choices, select the answer that is the best approximation. Then, fill in the appropriate oval on the answer sheet.

Notes:

1. A calculator will be needed to answer some of the questions on the test. Scientific, programmable, and graphing calculators are permitted. It is up to you to determine when and when not to use your calculator.
2. Angles on the Level 2 test are measured in degrees and radians. You need to decide whether your calculator should be set to degree mode or radian mode for a particular question.
3. Figures are drawn as accurately as possible and are intended to help solve some of the test problems. If a figure is not drawn to scale, this will be stated in the problem. All figures lie in a plane unless the problem indicates otherwise.
4. Unless otherwise stated, the domain of a function f is assumed to be the set of real numbers x for which the value of the function, $f(x)$, is a real number.
5. Reference information that may be useful in answering some of the test questions can be found below.

Reference Information
Right circular cone with radius r and height h: $\quad$ Volume $= \frac{1}{3}\pi r^2 h$
Right circular cone with circumference of base c and slant height ℓ: $\quad$ Lateral Area $= \frac{1}{2}c\ell$
Sphere with radius r: $\quad$ Volume $= \frac{4}{3}\pi r^3$ $\quad$ Surface Area $= 4\pi r^2$
Pyramid with base area B and height h: $\quad$ Volume $= \frac{1}{3}Bh$

PRACTICE TEST 6 QUESTIONS

USE THIS SPACE AS SCRATCH PAPER

1. The equation for a sphere passing through the origin is given by the equation $(x - 2)^2 + (y - 6)^2 + (z - k)^2 = 49$. What is a possible value of k?

   (A) 0
   (B) 1
   (C) 2
   (D) 3
   (E) 6

2. Which of the following is perpendicular to the line $y + 4x = 2$?

   (A) $y = -4x + 4$

   (B) $y = -\dfrac{1}{4}x - 2$

   (C) $y = x + 8$

   (D) $y = \dfrac{1}{4}x + 1$

   (E) $y = 2x - 4$

3. What is $\log_2 \dfrac{\sqrt{ab}}{c^3}$ in expanded form?

   (A) $\log_2 a + \log_2 b - \log_2 c$

   (B) $\log_{\frac{1}{2}} a + \log_{\frac{1}{2}} b - \log_3 c$

   (C) $\log 2a + \log 2b - \log 3c$

   (D) $\dfrac{3}{2}\log_2 a + \dfrac{3}{2}\log_2 b - \dfrac{1}{2}\log_2 c$

   (E) $\dfrac{1}{2}\log_2 a + \dfrac{1}{2}\log_2 b - 3\log_2 c$

4. Which is the standard form of the equation of the ellipse represented on the graph?

   (A) $\dfrac{x^2}{5} + \dfrac{y^2}{6} = 1$

   (B) $x^2 + y^2 = 30$

   (C) $\dfrac{x^2}{25} + \dfrac{y^2}{36} = 1$

   (D) $\dfrac{x^2}{10} + \dfrac{y^2}{12} = 1$

   (E) $\dfrac{x^2}{4} + \dfrac{y^2}{9} = 1$

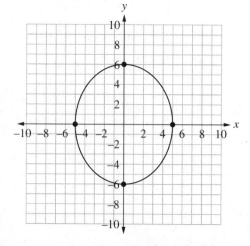

GO ON TO THE NEXT PAGE

5. How many real roots does $3x^2 - 2x + 4$ have?

    (A) 0 real solutions
    (B) 1 real solution
    (C) 2 real solutions
    (D) 3 real solutions
    (E) an infinite number of real solutions

6. Two six-sided number cubes are thrown. What is the probability of rolling a pair of 3s?

    (A) $\dfrac{1}{3}$

    (B) $\dfrac{1}{6}$

    (C) $\dfrac{1}{9}$

    (D) $\dfrac{1}{18}$

    (E) $\dfrac{1}{36}$

7. What is the product of $(2 + 3i)(1 - 4i)$?

    (A) $10 - 11i$
    (B) $14 - 5i$
    (C) $11i$
    (D) 14
    (E) $9 + 5i$

8. A circle has a radius of 12 centimeters. What is the area of a sector whose arc length is 8π centimeters?

    (A) 20π square centimeters
    (B) 24π square centimeters
    (C) 36π square centimeters
    (D) 48π square centimeters
    (E) 72π square centimeters

9. The distance between two points in space, $F(0, -1, 3)$ and $G(2, -2, b)$, is 3. Which is a possible value of b?

    (A) -2
    (B) -1
    (C) 0
    (D) 1
    (E) 3

GO ON TO THE NEXT PAGE

10. What is the value of cos θ in the triangle below?

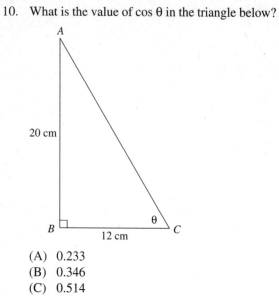

(A) 0.233
(B) 0.346
(C) 0.514
(D) 0.682
(E) 0.842

11. Which of the following lines are vertical asymptotes of the graph of $y = \dfrac{x+2}{x+1}$?

    I. $x = -1$
    II. $x = 0$
    III. $x = 1$

(A) I only
(B) II only
(C) III only
(D) I and III
(E) II and III

12. If $f(x) = \dfrac{x+2}{2x-3}$, then $f^{-1}(x)$ is

(A) $\dfrac{2x-1}{3x+2}$

(B) $\dfrac{3x+2}{2x-1}$

(C) $\dfrac{x-2}{2x+3}$

(D) $\dfrac{2x+3}{x-2}$

(E) $3x - 1$

13. The y-intercept of the line that passes through the points $(-1, -6)$ and $(1, 2)$ is

(A) -2

(B) $-\dfrac{1}{2}$

(C) $\dfrac{3}{2}$

(D) 4

(E) 8

GO ON TO THE NEXT PAGE

14. What are the coordinates of the vertex of the parabola whose equation is $y = 4x^2 - 16x + 2$?

    (A) $(-2, 10)$
    (B) $(-1, 14)$
    (C) $(1, 7)$
    (D) $(-2, -12)$
    (E) $(2, -14)$

USE THIS SPACE AS SCRATCH PAPER

15. Which of the following is a solution to $2x^2 + x < 6$?

    (A) $-2 < x < 1$
    (B) $-2 < x < \dfrac{3}{2}$
    (C) $-\dfrac{3}{2} < x < 2$
    (D) $-2 < x$
    (E) $x < -2$ or $x > \dfrac{3}{2}$

16. If $x^b \cdot (x^{b+2})^b \cdot (x^b)^{b-1} = x^k$, then $k =$

    (A) $2b^2 - b$
    (B) $b^2 + b$
    (C) $2b + 1$
    (D) $2b^2 + 2b$
    (E) $b^2 + 3b$

17. The sum of the zeros of $y = 2x^2 + 6x - 8$ is

    (A) -3
    (B) -2
    (C) 0
    (D) 4
    (E) 6

18. Which degree measure is equivalent to $\left(\dfrac{\pi}{2}\right)^R$?

    (A) $45°$
    (B) $90°$
    (C) $120°$
    (D) $180°$
    (E) $270°$

19. What is the determinant of $\begin{pmatrix} -6 & -2 \\ x & 1 \end{pmatrix}$?

    (A) $6 - 2x$
    (B) $12 - x$
    (C) $-6x - 2$
    (D) $2x - 6$
    (E) $x + 12$

GO ON TO THE NEXT PAGE

20. A committee of 4 people is to be selected from 5 men and 6 women. If the members of the committee are selected at random, what is the probability that the committee consists of 1 man and 3 women?

(A) $\dfrac{4}{11}$

(B) $\dfrac{1}{4}$

(C) $\dfrac{5}{101}$

(D) $\dfrac{10}{33}$

(E) $\dfrac{2}{73}$

21. Which function below could be represented by the graph?

(A) $y = 3 \sin x + 1$

(B) $y = \sin \dfrac{x}{2} + 1$

(C) $y = 2 \sin 2x + 1$

(D) $y = \dfrac{1}{2} \sin (x + 2)$

(E) $y = \sin x$

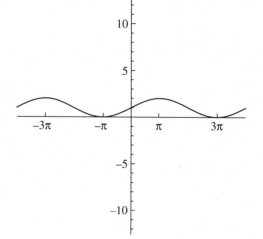

22. What the radius of a sphere whose center is at the origin that passes through the point (3, 2, 4)?

(A) 2.8
(B) 3.3
(C) 4.5
(D) 5.4
(E) 6.1

23. How can $\dfrac{(2^{-1}a^3b^{-2})^{-2}}{(4a^2b^{-1}c^{-2})^2}$ be expressed with only positive exponents?

(A) $\dfrac{1}{16a^{10}b^6c^4}$

(B) $\dfrac{b^6c^4}{4a^{10}}$

(C) $\dfrac{4a^{10}}{b^6c^4}$

(D) $\dfrac{a^2}{b^4c^2}$

(E) $\dfrac{1}{a^8b^4c^2}$

GO ON TO THE NEXT PAGE

24. If $x - 2$ is a factor of $x^4 + 3x^3 - 5x^2 + kx - 24$, what is the value of k?

(A) −5
(B) −2
(C) 2
(D) 7
(E) 14

25. The graph below has been transformed from its basic function. Which equation describes the function represented?

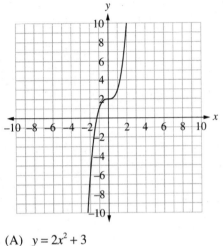

(A) $y = 2x^2 + 3$
(B) $y = \sqrt{x}$
(C) $y = 3|x| + 2$
(D) $y = x^3 + 2$
(E) $y = \sqrt{x} - 2$

26. You have a total of 18 video games. You are able to bring any 5 games on an overnight trip. How many ways can you choose the 5 games?

(A) 90
(B) 450
(C) 2160
(D) 4896
(E) 8568

27. What is cos 150° in terms of θ_r?

(A) −sin 150°
(B) −cos 30°
(C) cos 30°
(D) sin 50°
(E) cos 80°

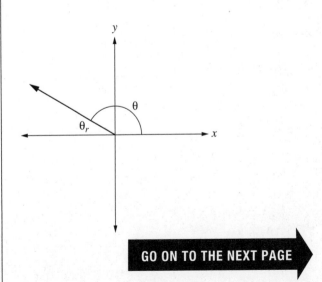

GO ON TO THE NEXT PAGE

28. $\log_3 12 =$

    (A) 0.44
    (B) 0.51
    (C) 0.60
    (D) 1.12
    (E) 2.26

29. The vertex angle of an isosceles triangle is 18°. If the length of the base is 6 centimeters, what is the perimeter of the triangle?

    (A) 19.18 cm
    (B) 33.77 cm
    (C) 38.35 cm
    (D) 44.35 cm
    (E) 57.53 cm

30. What is the distance from point $(-1, 4)$ to line $2x + y = 4$ to the nearest tenth?

    (A) 1.5
    (B) 1.2
    (C) 0.9
    (D) 0.7
    (E) 0.4

31. If $f(x) = \sqrt{x - 2}$ and $g(x) = 2x$, $(g \circ f)(x)$ equals

    (A) $2x^2 - 4$
    (B) $\dfrac{2}{\sqrt{2x - 2}}$
    (C) $\dfrac{\sqrt{2x - 2}}{2}$
    (D) $\sqrt{2x - 2}$
    (E) $2\sqrt{x - 2}$

32. If $A = \begin{pmatrix} 4 \\ -2 \\ 6 \end{pmatrix}$ and $B = (-1 \ \ 0 \ \ 3)$, what is AB?

    (A) $\begin{pmatrix} -4 & 12 \\ 2 & -6 \\ -6 & 18 \end{pmatrix}$

    (B) $\begin{pmatrix} -4 & 2 & 18 \\ 0 & 0 & -6 \\ 12 & 6 & 18 \end{pmatrix}$

    (C) $\begin{pmatrix} -4 & 0 & 12 \\ 2 & 0 & -6 \\ -6 & 0 & 18 \end{pmatrix}$

    (D) $\begin{pmatrix} -3 \\ 8 \\ -3 \end{pmatrix}$

    (E) $(4 \ \ 0 \ \ 18)$

GO ON TO THE NEXT PAGE

33. If $f(x) = -2x + 1$, what is $f(x - 4)$?

   (A) $2x + 5$
   (B) $10x$
   (C) $2x - 9$
   (D) $2x^2 + 9$
   (E) $9 - 2x$

34. If $f(x) = x^2 - 2x + 1$, then $f(h + 2) =$

   (A) $h^2 + 2h + 1$
   (B) $6h + 4$
   (C) $2h^2 + 6h + 1$
   (D) $h^2 + 3h$
   (E) $4h^2 - 2h + 4$

35. What is the length of the major axis of the ellipse whose equation is $25x^2 + 4y^2 = 100$?

   (A) 2
   (B) 5
   (C) 7
   (D) 10
   (E) 15

36. In a group of 300 people, 75 have type A blood, 96 have type B blood, 105 have type O blood, and 24 have type AB blood. What is the probability that a person selected at random has type O blood?

   (A) 0.35
   (B) 0.53
   (C) 0.72
   (D) 0.96
   (E) 1.05

37. What is the fifth term in the geometric sequence 1, 2, 4, …?

   (A) 8
   (B) 16
   (C) 18
   (D) 24
   (E) 26

38. The hour hand of a clock moves r radians in 24 minutes. What is the value of r?

   (A) 0.1
   (B) 0.3
   (C) 0.5
   (D) 1.2
   (E) 1.6

GO ON TO THE NEXT PAGE

USE THIS SPACE AS SCRATCH PAPER

39. If $f(x) = \dfrac{1}{x-2}$ and $g(x) = 3x$, what is $f \cdot g$?

    (A) $3x^2 - 6$

    (B) $\dfrac{-3x^2 - 6x + 1}{x - 2}$

    (C) $\dfrac{x - 2}{3x}$

    (D) $\dfrac{3x}{x - 2}$

    (E) $\dfrac{6x - 1}{x - 2}$

40. What is the domain of $f(x) = (5x - 2)^{\frac{3}{2}}$?

    (A) $\{x : x \neq -\dfrac{2}{5} \text{ and } x \neq \dfrac{2}{5}\}$

    (B) $\{x : x \geq \dfrac{2}{5}\}$

    (C) $\{x : x \leq \dfrac{2}{5}\}$

    (D) $\{x : x \geq 7\}$
    (E) $\{x : x \leq 7\}$

41. $x^{\frac{1}{3}} + x^{\frac{2}{3}} =$

    (A) x
    (B) $2x$

    (C) $\dfrac{1}{x^{\frac{1}{3}}}$

    (D) $x^{\frac{1}{3}}(1 + x^{\frac{1}{3}})$

    (E) $\dfrac{1}{x}$

42. To the nearest tenth, the positive zero of $y = 2x^2 + 5x - 4$ is

    (A) 0.6
    (B) 0.8
    (C) 0.9
    (D) 1.3
    (E) 3.1

43. Tina's Toy Shop has 24 mystery boxes to choose from. Eighteen are super-size and 6 are mini-size. If a shopper chooses two mystery boxes at random, what is the probability that both are super-size?

    (A) 0.24
    (B) 0.33
    (C) 0.48
    (D) 0.55
    (E) 0.63

GO ON TO THE NEXT PAGE

44. What is the domain of the function $g(x) = \dfrac{x+2}{18-3x-x^2}$?

(A) $\{x : x \le 0\}$

(B) $\{x : x \ge 1\}$

(C) $\{x : x \ne -6 \text{ and } x \ne 3\}$

(D) $\{x : x \ne -2 \text{ and } x \ne 18\}$

(E) all real numbers

45. The slope of the linear function, f, is 3. If $f(2) = 10$ and $f(-2) = n$, what is n?

(A) -2

(B) -1

(C) $-\dfrac{1}{2}$

(D) 2

(E) 6

46. Which point on the graph represents $4 - 2i$?

(A) A

(B) B

(C) C

(D) D

(E) E

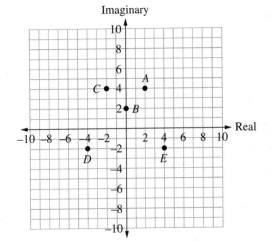

47. The graph of which equation has an amplitude of $\dfrac{1}{2}$?

(A) $y = \dfrac{3}{2}\sin\dfrac{x}{2}$

(B) $y = \dfrac{1}{2}\sin\dfrac{\pi}{2}$

(C) $y = 2\sin x$

(D) $y = \sin\dfrac{x}{2}$

(E) $y = \dfrac{5}{2}\sin\dfrac{5\pi}{2}$

GO ON TO THE NEXT PAGE

48. If point (x, y) is in the second quadrant, which of the following must be true?

     I. $x + y < 0$

     II. $x > y$

     III. $\dfrac{x}{y} > 0$

(A) I only
(B) II only
(C) III only
(D) I and II only
(E) No statements are true.

49. A point has rectangular coordinates (10, 10). The polar coordinates are $(14, \theta)$. What is θ?

(A) 37°
(B) 45°
(C) 62°
(D) 75°
(E) 90°

50. What is the smallest distance between point (1, 1) and a point on the circumference of the circle described by $(x - 4)^2 + (y + 3)^2 = 16$?

(A) 1
(B) 2
(C) 3
(D) 4
(E) 5

USE THIS SPACE AS SCRATCH PAPER

S T O P

IF YOU FINISH BEFORE TIME IS CALLED, YOU MAY CHECK YOUR WORK ON THIS TEST ONLY.
DO NOT TURN TO ANY OTHER TEST IN THIS BOOK.

ANSWER KEY

1. D	11. A	21. B	31. E	41. D
2. D	12. B	22. D	32. C	42. A
3. E	13. A	23. B	33. E	43. D
4. C	14. E	24. C	34. A	44. C
5. A	15. B	25. D	35. D	45. A
6. E	16. D	26. E	36. A	46. E
7. B	17. A	27. B	37. B	47. B
8. D	18. B	28. E	38. B	48. E
9. D	19. D	29. D	39. D	49. B
10. C	20. D	30. C	40. B	50. A

ANSWERS AND EXPLANATIONS

1. **(D)** The radius of the sphere is 7. Use the distance formula to find the value of k: $d = \sqrt{(2-0)^2 + (6-0)^2 + (k-0)^2} = \sqrt{4+36+k^2} = 7$. Square both sides of the equation to yield $40 + k^2 = 49$, so $k = 3$ or -3.

2. **(D)** Rewrite the equation in the form $y = -4x + 2$. The slope of the given line is -4. The slope of the line that is perpendicular is the negative reciprocal, or $\frac{1}{4}$.

3. **(E)** Use the properties of logarithms: $\log_2 \frac{\sqrt{ab}}{c^3} = \log_2 \frac{(ab)^{\frac{1}{2}}}{c^3} = \log_2(ab)^{\frac{1}{2}} - \log_2 c^3$, which becomes $\frac{1}{2}\log_2(ab) - 3\log_2 c$. Then $\frac{1}{2}(\log_2 a + \log_2 b) - 3\log_2 c$, which is $\frac{1}{2}\log_2 a + \frac{1}{2}\log_2 b - 3\log_2 c$.

4. **(C)** The ellipse can be described by the equation $\frac{x^2}{b^2} + \frac{y^2}{a^2} = 1$, $a = 6$ and $b = 5$.

5. **(A)** Determine the discriminant: $d = b^2 - 4ac = (-2)^2 - 4(3)(4) = 4 - 48 = -44$. If $d < 0$, the equation has zero real solutions.

6. **(E)** $P(\text{two 3s}) = P(3) \cdot P(3) = \frac{1}{6} \cdot \frac{1}{6} = \frac{1}{36}$.

7. **(B)** $(2 + 3i)(1 - 4i) = 2 - 8i + 3i - 12i^2 = i^2 = -1$, so the equation becomes $2 - 5i + 12$ which is $14 - 5i$.

8. **(D)** $s = r\theta$, $8\pi = 12\theta$ gives $\theta = \frac{2\pi}{3}$; $A = \frac{1}{2}r^2\theta = \frac{1}{2} \cdot 12^2 \cdot \frac{2\pi}{3} = 48\pi$.

9. **(D)** $d = \sqrt{(0-2)^2 + (-1-(-2))^2 + (3-b)^2} = 3$; Square both sides and simplify to get $(3-b)^2 = 4$. Solve for b. $(3-b) = z$ so $-b = -1$, or $b = 1$.

10. **(C)** Length of $AC = \sqrt{12^2 + 20^2} = \sqrt{544}$ cm, $\cos\theta = \frac{AB}{AC} = \frac{12}{\sqrt{544}} = 0.514$.

11. **(A)** The vertical asymptotes are the nonremovable values of x that make the denominator zero. Set the denominator equal to zero and solve. $x + 1 = 0$ so $x = -1$.

12. **(B)** Replace $f(x)$ with y. $f(x) = \frac{x+2}{2x-3}$ becomes $y = \frac{x+2}{2x-3}$. Then exchange x and y: $x = \frac{y+2}{2y-3}$. Solve for y: $x(2y-3) = y+2$; $2xy - 3x = y+2$; $2xy - y = 3x+2$; $y(2x-1) = 3x+2$; so $y = \frac{3x+2}{2x-1}$.

13. **(A)** The slope of the line is $\frac{-6-2}{-1-1}=\frac{-8}{-2}=4$. The point-slope equation is then $y+6=4(x+1)$. Solve for y to get $y=-4x-2$. The y-intercept of the line is -2.

14. **(E)** The x-coordinate is $x=-\frac{b}{2a}=-\frac{-16}{8}=2$. The y-coordinate is $y=4(2)^2-16(2)+2=-14$. Therefore, the vertex occurs at the point $(2, -14)$.

15. **(B)** $2x^2+x-6=(2x-3)(x+2)=0$ when $x=\frac{3}{2}$ or -2. Numbers between these values satisfy the inequality.

16. **(D)** $x^b \cdot x^{b^2+2b} \cdot x^{b^2-b} = x^{b+b^2+2b+b^2-b} = x^{2b^2+2b}$

17. **(A)** The sum of the zeros is $-\frac{b}{a}=-\frac{6}{2}=-3$. Another method is to find the solutions of the equation and add them.

18. **(B)** Multiply by $\frac{180°}{\pi}:\frac{\pi}{2^R}\left(\frac{180°}{\pi}\right)=90°$.

19. **(D)** The determinant of $\begin{pmatrix} a & b \\ c & d \end{pmatrix}$ is $ab-cd$. $(-6)(1)-(-2)(x)=-6+2x$.

20. **(D)** There are $\binom{11}{4}$ ways of selecting a committee of 4 members from 11 people. There are $\binom{5}{1}$ ways of selecting 1 man from 5, and there are $\binom{6}{3}$ ways of selecting 3 women from 6. Find that $\dfrac{\binom{5}{1}\binom{6}{3}}{\binom{11}{4}}=\dfrac{10}{33}$.

21. **(B)** The amplitude is 1, so you know that the coefficient of sin is 1. You also know that the graph is shifted up 1 unit. The period is 4π so the function must be $y=\sin\frac{x}{2}+1$.

22. **(D)** The radius is the distance from the center to any point on the sphere, so use the distance formula to calculate. $d=\sqrt{(3-0)^2+(2-0)^2+(4-0)^2}=\sqrt{29}\approx 5.4$.

23. **(B)** Begin by simplifying the top parentheses: $\dfrac{(2^{-1}a^3b^{-2})^{-2}}{(4a^2b^{-1}c^{-2})^2}=\dfrac{1}{(4a^2b^{-1}c^{-2})^2(2^{-1}a^3b^{-2})^2}$. Then apply the exponents outside the parentheses:

$\dfrac{1}{(16a^4b^{-2}c^{-4})(2^{-2}a^6b^{-4})}=\dfrac{1}{\left(\dfrac{16a^4}{b^2c^4}\right)\left(\dfrac{a^6}{2^2b^4}\right)}$. Simplify:

$\dfrac{1}{\left(\dfrac{16a^{10}}{4b^6c^4}\right)}=\dfrac{b^6c^4}{4a^{10}}$. Another method is to distribute the powers and remove the parenthesis $\dfrac{2^2a^{-6}b^4}{4^2a^4b^{-2}c^{-4}}$.

Simplify the coefficients by dividing $\dfrac{a^{-6}b^4}{4a^4b^{-2}c^{-4}}$. Move the variables to the make the exponents positive $\dfrac{b^4b^2c^4}{4a^4a^6}$. Eliminate duplicate variables by adding the exponents $\dfrac{b^4c^4}{4a^{10}}$.

24. **(C)** If $x-2$ is a factor, it should divide into the polynomial without a remainder. Use synthetic division to solve:

2	1	3	−5	k	−24
		2	10	10	$2k+20$
	5	5	$k+10$	$(2k-4)$

Set the remainder equal to 0 and solve for k: $2k-4=0$, so $k=2$.

25. **(D)** The basic function is $y=x^3$. The graph is shifted 2 units, so the function becomes $y=x^3+2$.

26. **(E)** The problem involves a combination because order does not matter. To find the answer, enter the values for $_{18}C_5$ in your calculator to solve or solve as $\dfrac{18!}{(18-5)!5!}$.

27. **(B)** $\theta_r=180°-150°=30°$. The cosine is negative in quadrant II, so $\cos 150°=-\cos 30°$.

28. **(E)** Use the change-of-base formula to find $\dfrac{\log 12}{\log 3}$ by entering the values on your calculator.

29. **(D)** The altitude from the vertex to the base bisects both the vertex angle and the base to form two congruent right triangles.

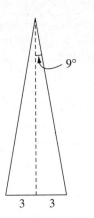

3   3

Therefore, $\sin 9° = \dfrac{3}{\text{leg}}$ and leg $= \dfrac{3}{\sin 9°} = 19.177$. The perimeter equals $19.177 + 19.177 + 6 = 44.35$ cm.

30. **(C)** Rewrite the equation for the line in the form $Ax + By + C = 0$: $2x + y - 4 = 0$. Then use the equation $d = \dfrac{|Ax_1 + By_1 + C|}{\sqrt{A^2 + B^2}}$. Therefore, $d = \dfrac{|2(-1) + (1)(4) - 4|}{\sqrt{2^2 + 1^2}}$, which simplifies to $\dfrac{2}{\sqrt{5}}$, or 0.9.

31. **(E)** $(g \circ f)(x) = g(f(x))$ so $g(f(x)) = 2\sqrt{x - 2}$.

32. **(C)** Multiply to find the product:

$\begin{pmatrix} (4 \cdot -1) + (0 \cdot 0) + (0 \cdot 0) & (4 \cdot 0) + (0 \cdot 0) + (0 \cdot 0) \\ (-2 \cdot -1) + (0 \cdot 0) + (0 \cdot 0) & (-2 \cdot 0) + (0 \cdot 0) + (0 \cdot 0) \\ (6 \cdot -1) + (0 \cdot 0) + (0 \cdot 0) & (6 \cdot 0) + (0 \cdot 0) + (0 \cdot 0) \end{pmatrix}$

$\begin{pmatrix} (4 \cdot 3) + (0 \cdot 0) + (0 \cdot 0) \\ (-2 \cdot 3) + (0 \cdot 0) + (0 \cdot 0) \\ (6 \cdot 3) + (0 \cdot 0) + (0 \cdot 0) \end{pmatrix}$. You can also do this on your graphing calculator.

33. **(E)** Replace x in the function with $x - 4$. $f(x - 4) = -2(x - 4) + 1 = -2x + 8 + 1 = -2x + 9$ which is $9 - 2x$.

34. **(A)** $f(h + 2)$ directs you to replace x with $h + 2$, and then simplify. Therefore, $f(h + 2) = (h + 2)^2 - 2(h + 2) + 1 = h^2 + 4h + 4 - 2h - 4 + 1 = h^2 + 2h + 1$.

35. **(D)** Write the equation in standard form by dividing both sides of the equation by 100 to get $\dfrac{x^2}{4} + \dfrac{y^2}{25} = 1$. Therefore, $a = 5$ and $b = 2$. The length of the major axis equals $2a = 10$.

36. **(A)** Compare the frequency of people with blood type O to the total number of frequencies: $\dfrac{105}{300} = 0.35$.

37. **(B)** $r = \dfrac{t_2}{t_1} = \dfrac{2}{1} = 2$ and $t_5 = t_1 r^{5-1}$ so $t_5 = 1 \cdot 2^4 = 16$.

38. **(B)** The hour hand of a clock moves $\dfrac{1}{12}$ of the way around the clock in 1 hour, or $\dfrac{2\pi}{12} = \dfrac{\pi}{6}$ radians. So $\dfrac{24}{60} \cdot \dfrac{\pi}{6} = \dfrac{\pi}{15} = .209$.

39. **(D)** $(f \cdot g)(x) = \dfrac{1}{x - 2} \cdot 3x = \dfrac{3x}{x - 2}$

40. **(B)** Determine the values of x that would make the radicand positive. $5x - 2 \geq 0$, so $x \geq \dfrac{2}{5}$.

41. **(D)** The exponents have the same bases. Factor out the greatest common factor, which is $x^{\frac{1}{3}}$.

$$x^{\frac{1}{3}} + x^{\frac{2}{3}} = x^{\frac{1}{3}}\left(1 + x^{\frac{1}{3}}\right)$$

42. **(A)** Enter the values into the quadratic formula program on your graphing calculator, or test answers in function. Choose the positive zero and round to the nearest tenth.

43. **(D)** The probability that the first selection is super-size is $\dfrac{18}{24}$. There are 23 boxes left, of which 17 are super-size. The probability that the second selection is also super-size is $\dfrac{18}{24} \cdot \dfrac{17}{23} = 0.55$.

44. **(C)** Factor the denominator and set it equal to zero. Find the values of x that will make the denominator zero. Exclude them from the domain.

45. **(A)** The line goes through the points $(2, 10)$ and $(-2, n)$. Use the formula to find the slope and then use the given slope to solve for b: $m = \dfrac{n - 10}{-2 - 2} = \dfrac{n - 10}{-4}$ and $\dfrac{n - 10}{-4} = 3$, so $n = -2$.

46. **(E)** Graph a complex number using rectangular coordinates by using the real part as the x-coordinate and the imaginary part as the y-coordinate.

47. **(B)** The amplitude is the coefficient of sin.

48. **(E)** The point must have a negative x-coordinate and a positive y-coordinate. That means that $x + y$ can be negative, positive, or equal to zero so I is not true. Because x is negative, it will always be less than y so II is not true. The fraction $\dfrac{x}{y}$ will always be negative so III is not true.

49. **(B)**

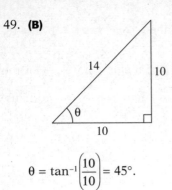

$$\theta = \tan^{-1}\left(\frac{10}{10}\right) = 45°.$$

50. **(A)** Use the equation to find that the center of the circle is at (4, –3) and the radius is 4. Then use the distance formula to find the distance from the center to point (5, –5). $d = \sqrt{(4-1)^2 + (-3-1)^2} = 5$. Finally, subtract the radius of the circle from the distance to the given point. So, $5 - 4 = 1$.

▨ DIAGNOSE YOUR STRENGTHS AND WEAKNESSES

Check the number of each question answered correctly and "X" the number of each question answered incorrectly.

Algebra and Functions	2	3	5	11	12	13	14	15	16	17	23	24	Total Number Correct
24 questions													
	25	28	30	31	33	34	39	40	41	42	44	45	

Trigonometry	8	10	18	21	27	29	38	47	Total Number Correct
8 questions									

Coordinate and Three-Dimensional Geometry	1	4	9	22	35	48	49	50	Total Number Correct
8 questions									

Numbers and Operations	7	19	26	32	37	46	Total Number Correct
6 questions							

Data Analysis, Statistics, and Probability	6	20	36	43	Total Number Correct
4 questions					

Number of correct answers $-\dfrac{1}{4}$ (Number of incorrect answers) = Your raw score

_____ $-\dfrac{1}{4}$ (_____) = _____

Compare your raw score with the approximate SAT Subject Test score below:

	Raw Score	SAT Subject Test Approximate Score
Excellent	43–50	770–800
Very Good	33–43	670–770
Good	27–33	620–670
Above Average	21–27	570–620
Average	11–21	500–570
Below Average	< 11	< 500

PRACTICE TEST 7

Treat this practice test as the actual test and complete it in one 60-minute sitting. Use the following answer sheet to fill in your multiple-choice answers. Once you have completed the practice test:

1. Check your answers using the Answer Key.
2. Review the Answers and Solutions.
3. Fill in the "Diagnose Your Strengths and Weaknesses" sheet, and determine areas that require further preparation.

PRACTICE TEST 7

MATH LEVEL 2

ANSWER SHEET

Tear out this answer sheet and use it to complete the practice test. Determine the BEST answer for each question. Then, fill in the appropriate oval using a No. 2 pencil.

1. (A) (B) (C) (D) (E)	21. (A) (B) (C) (D) (E)	41. (A) (B) (C) (D) (E)
2. (A) (B) (C) (D) (E)	22. (A) (B) (C) (D) (E)	42. (A) (B) (C) (D) (E)
3. (A) (B) (C) (D) (E)	23. (A) (B) (C) (D) (E)	43. (A) (B) (C) (D) (E)
4. (A) (B) (C) (D) (E)	24. (A) (B) (C) (D) (E)	44. (A) (B) (C) (D) (E)
5. (A) (B) (C) (D) (E)	25. (A) (B) (C) (D) (E)	45. (A) (B) (C) (D) (E)
6. (A) (B) (C) (D) (E)	26. (A) (B) (C) (D) (E)	46. (A) (B) (C) (D) (E)
7. (A) (B) (C) (D) (E)	27. (A) (B) (C) (D) (E)	47. (A) (B) (C) (D) (E)
8. (A) (B) (C) (D) (E)	28. (A) (B) (C) (D) (E)	48. (A) (B) (C) (D) (E)
9. (A) (B) (C) (D) (E)	29. (A) (B) (C) (D) (E)	49. (A) (B) (C) (D) (E)
10. (A) (B) (C) (D) (E)	30. (A) (B) (C) (D) (E)	50. (A) (B) (C) (D) (E)
11. (A) (B) (C) (D) (E)	31. (A) (B) (C) (D) (E)	
12. (A) (B) (C) (D) (E)	32. (A) (B) (C) (D) (E)	
13. (A) (B) (C) (D) (E)	33. (A) (B) (C) (D) (E)	
14. (A) (B) (C) (D) (E)	34. (A) (B) (C) (D) (E)	
15. (A) (B) (C) (D) (E)	35. (A) (B) (C) (D) (E)	
16. (A) (B) (C) (D) (E)	36. (A) (B) (C) (D) (E)	
17. (A) (B) (C) (D) (E)	37. (A) (B) (C) (D) (E)	
18. (A) (B) (C) (D) (E)	38. (A) (B) (C) (D) (E)	
19. (A) (B) (C) (D) (E)	39. (A) (B) (C) (D) (E)	
20. (A) (B) (C) (D) (E)	40. (A) (B) (C) (D) (E)	

PRACTICE TEST 7

Time: 60 minutes

Directions: Select the BEST answer for each of the 50 multiple-choice questions. If the exact solution is not one of the five choices, select the answer that is the best approximation. Then, fill in the appropriate oval on the answer sheet.

Notes:

1. A calculator will be needed to answer some of the questions on the test. Scientific, programmable, and graphing calculators are permitted. It is up to you to determine when and when not to use your calculator.
2. Angles on the Level 2 test are measured in degrees and radians. You need to decide whether your calculator should be set to degree mode or radian mode for a particular question.
3. Figures are drawn as accurately as possible and are intended to help solve some of the test problems. If a figure is not drawn to scale, this will be stated in the problem. All figures lie in a plane unless the problem indicates otherwise.
4. Unless otherwise stated, the domain of a function f is assumed to be the set of real numbers x for which the value of the function, $f(x)$, is a real number.
5. Reference information that may be useful in answering some of the test questions can be found below.

Reference Information	
Right circular cone with radius r and height h:	Volume $= \dfrac{1}{3}\pi r^2 h$
Right circular cone with circumference of base c and slant height ℓ:	Lateral Area $= \dfrac{1}{2}c\ell$
Sphere with radius r:	Volume $= \dfrac{4}{3}\pi r^3$ Surface Area $= 4\pi r^2$
Pyramid with base area B and height h:	Volume $= \dfrac{1}{3}Bh$

▰ PRACTICE TEST 7 QUESTIONS

USE THIS SPACE AS SCRATCH PAPER

1. A school uniform consists of 3 different shirts, 2 different pants, and 3 different pairs of socks. If any shirt, pants, and socks can be worn together, how many different combinations can be made?

    (A) 5
    (B) 7
    (C) 12
    (D) 18
    (E) 21

2. A player spins both spinners shown. What is the probability of spinning an odd number with the letter B?

    (A) $\dfrac{2}{5}$

    (B) $\dfrac{3}{5}$

    (C) $\dfrac{2}{3}$

    (D) $\dfrac{1}{5}$

    (E) $\dfrac{2}{15}$

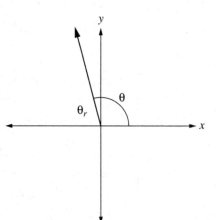

3. What is cos 105° in terms of θ_r?

    (A) cos 185°
    (B) cos 75°
    (C) cos 40°
    (D) −cos 75°
    (E) −cos 105°

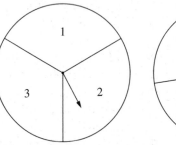

4. If $x = 2 - 3i$, $x^2 =$

    (A) $-5 - 12i$
    (B) $6 - i$
    (C) $1 + 6i$
    (D) $-1 + i$
    (E) $5 - i$

5. Two cards are drawn from a regular deck of 52 cards at random. What is the probability that both will be aces?

    (A) 0.002
    (B) 0.005
    (C) 0.031
    (D) 0.059
    (E) 0.077

GO ON TO THE NEXT PAGE

6. If $4x + 3y = 2$ and $3x + 4y = 5$, what is $x - y$?

(A) -3
(B) -1
(C) 0
(D) 3
(E) 7

7. How can $\dfrac{a^{-3} + a^{-1}}{ab^{-1}}$ be expressed with only positive exponents?

(A) $\dfrac{2b}{a^6}$

(B) $\dfrac{b}{a^2}\left(\dfrac{1}{a^2} + 1\right)$

(C) $\dfrac{1}{ab^2} + 1$

(D) $\dfrac{b}{a^2} + \dfrac{1}{a^3}$

(E) $\dfrac{ab}{a^3 + a^1}$

8. If $x + 2$ is a factor of $x^3 + 2x^2 + kx + 2$, what is the value of k?

(A) -3
(B) -1
(C) 1
(D) 3
(E) 6

9. $x^2 + x^3 =$

(A) x^5
(B) x
(C) $x^2(1 + x)$
(D) $\dfrac{x^2}{x^3}$
(E) $2x^6$

10. Which of the following functions transforms $y = f(x)$ by moving it 3 units to the left?

(A) $y = f(x + 3)$
(B) $y = f(x - 3)$
(C) $y = f(x) + 3$
(D) $y = f(x) - 3$
(E) $y = 3f(x)$

GO ON TO THE NEXT PAGE

11. If the triangle below is rotated 360° about the axis *AB*, what is the surface area of the resulting solid?

(A) 4π
(B) 6π
(C) 8π
(D) 12π
(E) 16π

12. Which of the following is perpendicular to the line $2y + x = -2$?

(A) $y = -x + 2$

(B) $y = \dfrac{1}{4}x - 2$

(C) $y = -\dfrac{1}{2}x + 4$

(D) $y = \dfrac{1}{2}x + 1$

(E) $y = 2x + 4$

13. Which of the following describes the vertical asymptotes of the graph of $y = \dfrac{x-3}{x^2+4}$?

(A) $x = -2$ or 2
(B) $x = 0$
(C) $x = 2$ or -4
(D) $x = 3$
(E) There are no vertical asymptotes.

14. What are the coordinates of the vertex of the parabola whose equation is $y = 2x^2 - 4x + 6$?

(A) $(1, -4)$
(B) $(-1, 4)$
(C) $(1, 4)$
(D) $(-1, -4)$
(E) $(4, -1)$

GO ON TO THE NEXT PAGE

15. Which of the following is equivalent to $\log_b \sqrt[3]{x^2 y}$?

    (A) $\dfrac{2}{3}\log_b x + \dfrac{1}{3}\log_b y$

    (B) $\log_b 2x + \log_b 3y$

    (C) $\dfrac{1}{3}\log_b 6x$

    (D) $\dfrac{1}{3}\log_b x + \dfrac{1}{3}\log_b y$

    (E) $\dfrac{1}{3}\log_b x + \log_b y$

16. If $f(x) = \dfrac{1}{x}$ and $g(x) = 2x$, $(f-g)(x)$ equals

    (A) $\dfrac{1-2x}{x}$

    (B) $\dfrac{1}{x - x^2}$

    (C) $\dfrac{2x - 4}{x^2 - 4x}$

    (D) $\dfrac{1 - 2x^2}{x}$

    (E) 2

17. The y-intercept of the line that passes through the points $(-3, 4)$ and $(9, 8)$ is

    (A) -9
    (B) -4
    (C) $\dfrac{3}{2}$
    (D) 5
    (E) 8

18. A student scored 89, 92, 84, 86, and 90 on 5 quizzes. If they are equally weighted, what must the student score on the next quiz to have an average of 90?

    (A) 92
    (B) 94
    (C) 95
    (D) 99
    (E) 100

19. The 8th term of the sequence 2, 6, 18, 54, …

    (A) 480
    (B) 640
    (C) 972
    (D) 1458
    (E) 4374

GO ON TO THE NEXT PAGE

20. Which complex number has a modulus of 5?

    (A) $2 - 3i$
    (B) $3 + 5i$
    (C) $1 + 6i$
    (D) $4 + 3i$
    (E) $2 + 2i$

USE THIS SPACE AS SCRATCH PAPER

21. Which is the equation of a circle that has a diameter with endpoints at $A(-5, 3)$ and $B(1, 3)$?

    (A) $(x - 1)^2 + (y - 3)^2 = 25$
    (B) $(x + 2)^2 + (y - 3)^2 = 9$
    (C) $(x - 5)^2 + (y - 3)^2 = 9$
    (D) $(x + 3)^2 + (y + 2)^2 = 3$
    (E) $(x - 2)^2 + (y + 1)^2 = 6$

22. What is the perimeter of the triangle below?

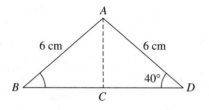

    (A) 27.6 cm
    (B) 21.2 cm
    (C) 20.1 cm
    (D) 18.4 cm
    (E) 9.2 cm

23. The slope of the linear function, f, is $-\dfrac{3}{2}$. If $f(2) = -4$ and $f(4) = z$, what is z?

    (A) -10
    (B) -7
    (C) -3
    (D) 2
    (E) 9

24. What is the radius of a sphere with the center at the origin that passes through the point $(2, 2, 2)$?

    (A) 2
    (B) 2.45
    (C) 2.83
    (D) 3.46
    (E) 4

25. If $f(x) = 2x^2 + 3x - 2$, then $f(3h + 1) =$

    (A) $18h^2 + 21h + 3$
    (B) $9h + 3$
    (C) $9h^2 + 6h + 1$
    (D) $6h^2 + 3h$
    (E) $4h^2 + 3h + 1$

GO ON TO THE NEXT PAGE

26. $\log_8 16 =$

    (A) 0.64
    (B) 0.75
    (C) 1.33
    (D) 1.82
    (E) 2.12

USE THIS SPACE AS SCRATCH PAPER

27. Which set of data values has the greatest range?

    (A) {56, 56, 56, 56}
    (B) {4, 9, 15, 26}
    (C) {87, 92, 93, 93}
    (D) {28, 30, 32, 34}
    (E) {50, 55, 60, 65}

28. If $f(x) = -x^2 + 9$, then $f^{-1}(x)$ is

    (A) $x^2 - 9$
    (B) $\sqrt{9 - x}$
    (C) $9 - x$
    (D) $x - 9$
    (E) $3x - 1$

29. If, $2X + \begin{pmatrix} -3 & 2 \\ 1 & 4 \end{pmatrix} = \begin{pmatrix} -5 & 6 \\ 7 & 4 \end{pmatrix}$, then $X =$

    (A) $\begin{pmatrix} -1 & 2 \\ 3 & 0 \end{pmatrix}$

    (B) $\begin{pmatrix} -2 & 4 \\ 6 & 0 \end{pmatrix}$

    (C) $\begin{pmatrix} \dfrac{3}{2} & 1 \\ 1 & 0 \end{pmatrix}$

    (D) $\begin{pmatrix} -6 & 4 \\ 1 & 8 \end{pmatrix}$

    (E) $\begin{pmatrix} -10 & 12 \\ 14 & 8 \end{pmatrix}$

30. A ramp leads up to a bridge as shown. What is the height of the bridge?

    (A) 200 ft
    (B) 225 ft
    (C) 250 ft
    (D) 300 ft
    (E) 450 ft

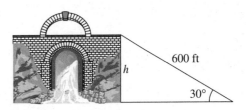

GO ON TO THE NEXT PAGE

31. If $x - 1$ and $x + 3$ are both factors of $x^3 + 6x^2 + bx - 12$, then b must be

    (A) −4
    (B) −1
    (C) 3
    (D) 5
    (E) 12

USE THIS SPACE AS SCRATCH PAPER

32. What is the length of the minor axis of the ellipse whose equation is $7x^2 + y^2 = 7$?

    (A) 2
    (B) $\sqrt{7}$
    (C) 4
    (D) 7
    (E) 8

33. Which is the product of $(-2 + 3i)(1 - 4i)$ in standard form?

    (A) $3i$
    (B) $10 + 11i$
    (C) $-3 + 12i$
    (D) $-2 + i$
    (E) $1 + 2i$

34. If point $P(6, 8)$ lies on the terminal side of $\angle\theta$ in standard position, $\sin\theta =$

    (A) $\dfrac{4}{5}$

    (B) $\dfrac{3}{4}$

    (C) $\dfrac{5}{4}$

    (D) $\dfrac{4}{3}$

    (E) $\dfrac{3}{5}$

35. What is the distance between two points in space, $A(4, -2, 1)$ and $B(1, 0, 3)$?

    (A) 2.3
    (B) 3.7
    (C) 4.1
    (D) 4.8
    (E) 5.2

36. $\tan^{-1}(\tan 102°) =$

    (A) −89°
    (B) −78°
    (C) 78°
    (D) 89°
    (E) none of these

GO ON TO THE NEXT PAGE

37. $(x^2 + 3x + 1)(2x^3 - 3x^2 + x - 4) =$

(A) $x^5 - 2x^4 + 2x^3 - 4x^2 + 11x - 4$
(B) $2x^5 + 3x^4 - 6x^3 - 4x^2 - 11x - 4$
(C) $3x^5 - 3x^4 + 6x^3 + 4x^2 + x - 4$
(D) $x^5 - 2x^4 + 3x^3 - 2x^2 - 12x - 4$
(E) $2x^5 - 3x^4 + x^3 - 4x^2 - 12x + 1$

USE THIS SPACE AS SCRATCH PAPER

38. The area of the triangle shown is

(A) 68.8
(B) 72.1
(C) 79.8
(D) 80.0
(E) 85.8

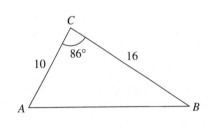

39. What is the distance from point $(2, 5)$ to line $3x - 2y = -6$ to the nearest 10th?

(A) 3.6
(B) 1.8
(C) 1.4
(D) 0.6
(E) 0.2

40. If $\log(\log x) = 1$, then $x =$

(A) 10
(B) 1000
(C) 100,000
(D) 100,000,000
(E) 10,000,000,000

41. What is the domain of $f(x) = \dfrac{x-1}{\sqrt{x+4}}$?

(A) $\{x : x \neq -4 \text{ and } x \neq 4\}$
(B) $\{x : x \geq 0\}$
(C) $\{x : x < -4\}$
(D) $\{x : x > -4\}$
(E) all real numbers

42. If a circle has a radius of 15, the area of a sector with a central angle of 60° to the nearest whole number is

(A) 17
(B) 45
(C) 75
(D) 92
(E) 118

GO ON TO THE NEXT PAGE

43. If the graph of $-x + 2y + 3 = 0$ is perpendicular to the graph of $ax + 3y - 1 = 0$, then $a =$

   (A) -3

   (B) $-\dfrac{2}{3}$

   (C) $\dfrac{1}{3}$

   (D) $\dfrac{3}{2}$

   (E) 6

USE THIS SPACE AS SCRATCH PAPER

44. Milana puts $1000 into a bank account that offers a 3.6% interest rate compounded monthly. How much money will be in the account 2 years later?

   (A) $1036.00

   (B) $1072.00

   (C) $1074.54

   (D) $2336.87

   (E) $2654.90

45. If $f(x) = 2x^3 + x^2 - x + 4$, then $f(i) =$

   (A) $-3i$

   (B) $3 - 3i$

   (C) $2i + 1$

   (D) $1 - 3i$

   (E) $2i + 4$

46. To the nearest 10th, the positive zero of $y = 4x^2 - 2x - 1$ is

   (A) 0.3

   (B) 0.6

   (C) 0.8

   (D) 1.1

   (E) 2.3

47. How many integers satisfy the inequality $x^2 - 2x < 8$?

   (A) 0

   (B) 2

   (C) 3

   (D) 5

   (E) an infinite number

GO ON TO THE NEXT PAGE

48. A student rolls 2 dice. What is the probability that the student will roll a pair?

    (A) $\dfrac{1}{12}$

    (B) $\dfrac{1}{10}$

    (C) $\dfrac{1}{8}$

    (D) $\dfrac{1}{6}$

    (E) $\dfrac{1}{3}$

49. If the slope of a line containing the points $(4, -1)$ and $(x, -4)$ is 0.25, x is

    (A) -8
    (B) -4
    (C) 1
    (D) 4
    (E) 12

50. If (a, b) is a solution to the system of equations $\begin{cases} 3x - y = 12 \\ x + 2y = 11 \end{cases}$, then the difference $a - b$ equals

    (A) -5
    (B) -2
    (C) 0
    (D) 2
    (E) 8

USE THIS SPACE AS SCRATCH PAPER

S T O P

IF YOU FINISH BEFORE TIME IS CALLED, YOU MAY CHECK YOUR WORK ON THIS TEST ONLY.
DO NOT TURN TO ANY OTHER TEST IN THIS BOOK.

ANSWER KEY

1. D	11. D	21. B	31. D	41. D
2. E	12. E	22. B	32. A	42. E
3. D	13. E	23. B	33. B	43. E
4. A	14. C	24. D	34. A	44. D
5. B	15. A	25. A	35. C	45. B
6. A	16. D	26. C	36. B	46. C
7. B	17. D	27. B	37. B	47. D
8. C	18. D	28. B	38. C	48. D
9. C	19. E	29. A	39. D	49. A
10. A	20. D	30. D	40. E	50. D

ANSWERS AND EXPLANATIONS

1. **(D)** Each of 3 shirts can go with each of 2 pants, which makes 6 combinations. Each of those combinations can go with each pair of socks, so $6 \cdot 3 = 18$ combinations.

2. **(E)** $P(\text{odd}) = \frac{2}{3}$ and $P(B) = \frac{1}{5}$. Therefore, the probability of spinning an even number with B is $\left(\frac{2}{3}\right)\left(\frac{1}{5}\right) = \frac{2}{15}$.

3. **(D)** $\theta_r = 180° - 105° = 75°$. The cos is negative in quadrant II, so $\cos 105° = -\cos 75°$.

4. **(A)** Enter the expression into your graphing calculator and push enter. An alternative method is to multiply the two binomials, remembering that $i^2 = -1$.
$(2 - 3i)(2 - 3i)$
$4 - 6i - 6i + 9i^2$
$4 - 12i - 9$
$-5 - 12i$

5. **(B)** There are 4 aces in a deck, so $P(\text{drawing an ace on the first card}) = \frac{4}{52} = \frac{1}{13}$. Once the card is removed, there are 3 aces out of 51 cards. Therefore, $P(\text{drawing an ace on the second card}) = \frac{3}{51} = \frac{1}{17}$. Multiply to find that $P(\text{drawing two aces}) = \frac{1}{13} \cdot \frac{1}{17} = \frac{1}{221} \approx 0.005$.

6. **(A)** Subtract the equations: $(4x + 3y) - (3x + 4y) = 2 - 5$, which becomes $x - y = -3$.

7. **(B)** Rewrite as: $\dfrac{a^{-3} + a^{-1}}{ab^{-1}} = \dfrac{\frac{1}{a^3} + \frac{1}{a}}{\frac{a}{b}}$. Then multiply by the reciprocal of the denominator: $\dfrac{b}{a}\left(\dfrac{1}{a^3} + \dfrac{1}{a}\right) = \dfrac{b}{a^4} + \dfrac{b}{a^2}$. Factor: $\dfrac{b}{a^2}\left(\dfrac{1}{a^2} + 1\right)$.

8. **(C)** If $x + 2$ is a factor, it should divide into the polynomial without a remainder. Use synthetic division to solve:

−2	1	2	k	2
		−2	0	−2k
	1	0	k	−2k + 2

Set the remainder equal to 0 and solve for k: $-2k + 2 = 0$, so $k = 1$.

9. **(C)** Factor out the greatest common factor, which is x^2. Therefore, $x^2 + x^3 = x^2(1 + x^1)$, which is $x^2(1 + x)$.

10. **(A)** The function $g(x)$ is translated as $g(x + c)$ to the right if $c < 0$ and to the left if $c > 0$. $c = 3$, so the function described by A is translated 3 units to the left.

11. **(D)** Sketch the resulting solid.

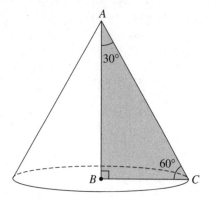

The lateral height of the cone is the hypotenuse of the triangle, which is 4. The radius is equal to the length of BC. $\sin 30 = \dfrac{BC}{4}$, $BC = 4 \sin 30 = 2$. Now substitute the values into the formula for the surface area of a cone: $SA = \pi r^2 + \pi r l = \pi(2)^2 + \pi(2)(4) = 4\pi + 8\pi = 12\pi$.

12. **(E)** Rewrite the equation in the form $y = -\dfrac{1}{2}x - 1$. The slope of the given line is $-\dfrac{1}{2}$. The slope of the line that is perpendicular is the negative reciprocal, or 2. The only equation with a slope of 2 is E.

13. **(E)** The vertical asymptotes are the nonremovable values of x that make the denominator 0. There are no values of x that make $x^2 + 4 = 0$, so there are no vertical asymptotes.

14. **(C)** The x-coordinate is $x = -\dfrac{b}{2a} = \dfrac{-4}{4} = 1$. The y-coordinate is $y = 2(1)^2 - 4(1) + 6 = 4$. Therefore, the vertex occurs at the point (1, 4).

15. **(A)** Use the properties of logarithms:, $\log_b \sqrt[3]{x^2 y} = \log_2 (x^2 y)^{\frac{1}{3}}$, which becomes $\dfrac{1}{3}\log_b (x^2 y)$. Then $\dfrac{1}{3}(\log_b x^2 + \log_b y)$, which is $\dfrac{2}{3}\log_b x + \dfrac{1}{3}\log_b y$.

16. **(D)** $(f - g)(x) = f(x) - g(x) = \dfrac{1}{x} - 2x = \dfrac{1}{x} - \dfrac{2x^2}{x} = \dfrac{1 - 2x^2}{x}$.

17. **(D)** The slope of the line is $\dfrac{4 - 8}{-3 - 9} = \dfrac{-4}{-12} = \dfrac{1}{3}$. The point-slope equation is then $y - 4 = \dfrac{1}{3}(x + 3)$. Solve for y to get $y = \dfrac{1}{3}x + 5$. The y-intercept of the line is 5.

18. **(D)** $\dfrac{89 + 92 + 84 + 86 + 90 + x}{6} = 90$, so $x = 99$.

19. **(E)** The sequence is geometric in which $n = 8$, $a_1 = 2$, and $r = 3$. The 8th term is $a_8 = 2 \cdot 3^{8-1} = 4{,}374$.

20. **(D)** The modulus of $a + bi$ is $\sqrt{a^2 + b^2}$. Evaluate each choice to find that only $4 + 3i$ results in $\sqrt{4^2 + 3^2} = \sqrt{25} = 5$.

21. **(B)** Use the midpoint formula to find the center of the circle. $\left(\dfrac{-5 + 1}{2}, \dfrac{3 + 3}{2}\right) = (-2, 3)$. Then find half the length of the diameter to determine the radius: $d = \dfrac{1}{2}\sqrt{(-5 - 1)^2 + (3 - 3)^2} = 3$. Insert the information into the standard equation for a circle: $(x + 2)^2 + (y - 3)^2 = 9$.

22. **(B)** The triangle is isosceles. The altitude therefore bisects the triangle to form two congruent right triangles. Determine the length of DC. $\cos 40° = \dfrac{DC}{6}$, so $DC = 6 \cos 40° = 4.596$. Therefore, $BD = 2DC = 9.2$. So the perimeter equals $9.2 + 6 + 6 = 21.2$ cm.

23. **(B)** The line goes through the points (2, –4) and (4, z). Use the formula to find the slope and then use the given slope to solve for b: $m = \dfrac{z - (-4)}{4 - 2} = \dfrac{z + 4}{2}$ and $\dfrac{z + 4}{2} = -\dfrac{3}{2}$, so $z = -7$.

24. **(D)** Use the distance formula to find the radius of the sphere: $d = \sqrt{(2 - 0)^2 + (2 - 0)^2 + (2 - 0)^2} = \sqrt{12}$. Use your calculator to find that $r \approx 3.46$.

25. **(A)** $f(3h + 1)$ directs you to replace x with $3h + 1$, and then simplify. Therefore, $f(3h + 1) = 2(3h + 1)^2 + 3(3h + 1) - 2 = 2(9h^2 + 6h + 1) + 9h + 3 - 2 = 18h^2 + 21h + 3$.

26. **(C)** Use the change-of-base formula to find $\dfrac{\log 16}{\log 8}$ by entering the values on your calculator.

27. **(B)** The range is the spread of the data. To find the range of each set, subtract the lowest value from the greatest value.

28. **(B)** Replace $f(x)$ with y. $f(x) = -x^2 + 9$ becomes $y = -x^2 + 9$. Then interchange x and y: $x = -y^2 + 9$. Solve for y: $x - 9 = -y^2$; $-x + 9 = y^2$; so $y = \sqrt{9 - x}$.

29. **(A)** $2X = \begin{pmatrix} -5 & 6 \\ 7 & 4 \end{pmatrix} - \begin{pmatrix} -3 & 2 \\ 1 & 4 \end{pmatrix} = \begin{pmatrix} -2 & 4 \\ 6 & 0 \end{pmatrix}$, so $X = \begin{pmatrix} -1 & 2 \\ 3 & 0 \end{pmatrix}$.

30. **(D)** Based on the diagram, $\sin 30° = \dfrac{h}{600}$ so $h = 600(\sin 30°) = 600\,(0.5) = 300$ ft.

31. **(D)** If $x - 1$ is a factor, $P(1) = (1)^3 + 6(1)^2 + b(1) - 12 = 0$, so $b = 5$.

32. **(A)** Write the equation in standard from by dividing both sides of the equation by 7 to get $\dfrac{x^2}{1} + \dfrac{y^2}{7} = 1$. Therefore, $a = \sqrt{7}$ and $b = 1$. The length of the minor axis equals $2b = 2$.

33. **(B)** The fastest method is to enter the problem into your calculator. Use 2nd decimal to enter i. Alternatively, you can use the foil method to multiply and remember to replace i^2 with -1.

$(-2 + 3i)(1 - 4i)$
$-2 + 8i + 3i - 12i^2$
$-2 + 11i + 12$
$10 + 11i$

34. **(A)** It is most useful to draw a diagram to solve the problem.

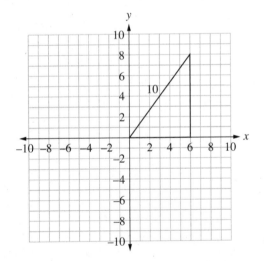

Use the Pythagorean Theorem to calculate the length of the hypotenuse as 10. Therefore, $\sin \theta = \dfrac{8}{10} = \dfrac{4}{5}$.

35. **(C)** Use the distance formula in three dimensions: $d = \sqrt{(4-1)^2 + (-2-0)^2 + (1-3)^2} = \sqrt{17} \approx 4.1$.

36. **(B)** Enter 2nd tan tan 102° into your calculator set to degrees.

37. **(B)** $(x^2 + 3x + 1)(2x^3 - 3x^2 + x - 4) = 2x^5 - 3x^4 + x^3 - 4x^2 + 6x^4 - 9x^3 + 3x^2 - 12x + 2x^3 - 3x^2 + x - 4 = 2x^5 + 3x^4 - 6x^3 - 4x^2 - 11x - 4$.

38. **(C)** $A = \dfrac{1}{2}ab \cdot \sin C = \dfrac{1}{2}(10)(16)(0.998) \approx 79.84$.

39. **(D)** Rewrite the equation for the line in the form $Ax + By + C = 0$: $3x - 2y + 6 = 0$. Then use the equation $d = \dfrac{|Ax_1 + By_1 + C|}{\sqrt{A^2 + B^2}}$. Therefore, $d = \dfrac{|3(2) + (-2)(5) + 6|}{\sqrt{3^2 + (-2)^2}}$, which simplifies to $\dfrac{2}{\sqrt{13}}$, or 0.55.

40. **(E)** If log (log x) = 1, so log x = 10. Therefore $x = 10^{10}$, or 10,000,000,000.

41. **(D)** Determine the values of x that would make the radicand negative or zero. Factor: $x + 4 > 0$.

42. **(E)** $A = \left(\dfrac{\theta}{360}\right)\pi r^2 = \left(\dfrac{60}{360}\right)\pi 15^2 \approx 117.8$.

An alternate method is to determine that the sector is $\dfrac{1}{6}$ of the total area of the circle. Therefore, calculating the area and finding $\dfrac{1}{6}$ will provide the same result.

43. **(E)** Rewrite the equations in the form $y = mx + b$ to find the slope of each equation. The slope of the first equation is $\dfrac{1}{2}$ and the slope of the second equation is $-\dfrac{a}{3}$. To be perpendicular, one slope must be the negative reciprocal of the other. Therefore, $-\dfrac{a}{3} = -2$, so $a = 6$.

44. **(D)** Interest compounded monthly means that it will compound 24 times in the 2-year period.

$P\left(1 + \dfrac{r}{12}\right)^{24} = 000\left(1 + \dfrac{.036}{12}\right)^{24} = 1074.54$.

45. **(B)** Enter $f(i) = 2i^3 + i^2 - i + 4$ into your graphing calculator.

46. **(C)** Enter the values into the quadratic formula program on your graphing calculator, or test answers in function. Choose the positive zero and round to the nearest 10th.

47. **(D)** $x^2 - 2x - 8 = (x - 4)(x + 2) = 0$ when $x = 4$ or -2. Numbers between these values satisfy the inequality.

48. **(D)** There are 36 elements in the sample space. Of those, 6 elements are pairs. Therefore, the probability is $\frac{6}{36}$ or $\frac{1}{6}$.

49. **(A)** $m = \dfrac{-4 - (-1)}{x - 4} = \dfrac{-3}{x - 4} = \dfrac{1}{4}$, so $x - 4 = -12$. Therefore, $x = -8$.

50. **(D)** Solve the system of equations by solving one equation for y, and then substituting it into the other equation to solve for x, which gives the solution as $(5, 3)$. Then subtract to find the difference.

▬ DIAGNOSE YOUR STRENGTHS AND WEAKNESSES

Check the number of each question answered correctly and "X" the number of each question answered incorrectly.

Algebra and Functions	6	7	8	9	12	13	14	15	16	17	23	25	26	Total Number Correct
26 questions														
	28	31	37	39	40	41	43	44	45	46	47	49	50	

Trigonometry	3	22	30	34	36	38	42	Total Number Correct
7 questions								

Coordinate and Three-Dimensional Geometry	10	11	21	24	32	35	Total Number Correct
6 questions							

Numbers and Operations	1	4	19	20	29	33	Total Number Correct
6 questions							

Data Analysis, Statistics, and Probability	2	5	18	27	48	Total Number Correct
5 questions						

Number of correct answers $-\dfrac{1}{4}$ **(Number of incorrect answers) = Your raw score**

_____ $-\dfrac{1}{4}$ (_____) = _____

Compare your raw score with the approximate SAT Subject Test score below:

	Raw Score	SAT Subject Test Approximate Score
Excellent	43–50	770–800
Very Good	33–43	670–770
Good	27–33	620–670
Above Average	21–27	570–620
Average	11–21	500–570
Below Average	< 11	< 500

PRACTICE TEST 8

Treat this practice test as the actual test and complete it in one 60-minute sitting. Use the following answer sheet to fill in your multiple-choice answers. Once you have completed the practice test:

1. Check your answers using the Answer Key.
2. Review the Answers and Solutions.
3. Fill in the "Diagnose Your Strengths and Weaknesses" sheet, and determine areas that require further preparation.

PRACTICE TEST 8

MATH LEVEL 2

ANSWER SHEET

Tear out this answer sheet and use it to complete the practice test. Determine the BEST answer for each question. Then, fill in the appropriate oval using a No. 2 pencil.

1. Ⓐ Ⓑ Ⓒ Ⓓ Ⓔ	21. Ⓐ Ⓑ Ⓒ Ⓓ Ⓔ	41. Ⓐ Ⓑ Ⓒ Ⓓ Ⓔ
2. Ⓐ Ⓑ Ⓒ Ⓓ Ⓔ	22. Ⓐ Ⓑ Ⓒ Ⓓ Ⓔ	42. Ⓐ Ⓑ Ⓒ Ⓓ Ⓔ
3. Ⓐ Ⓑ Ⓒ Ⓓ Ⓔ	23. Ⓐ Ⓑ Ⓒ Ⓓ Ⓔ	43. Ⓐ Ⓑ Ⓒ Ⓓ Ⓔ
4. Ⓐ Ⓑ Ⓒ Ⓓ Ⓔ	24. Ⓐ Ⓑ Ⓒ Ⓓ Ⓔ	44. Ⓐ Ⓑ Ⓒ Ⓓ Ⓔ
5. Ⓐ Ⓑ Ⓒ Ⓓ Ⓔ	25. Ⓐ Ⓑ Ⓒ Ⓓ Ⓔ	45. Ⓐ Ⓑ Ⓒ Ⓓ Ⓔ
6. Ⓐ Ⓑ Ⓒ Ⓓ Ⓔ	26. Ⓐ Ⓑ Ⓒ Ⓓ Ⓔ	46. Ⓐ Ⓑ Ⓒ Ⓓ Ⓔ
7. Ⓐ Ⓑ Ⓒ Ⓓ Ⓔ	27. Ⓐ Ⓑ Ⓒ Ⓓ Ⓔ	47. Ⓐ Ⓑ Ⓒ Ⓓ Ⓔ
8. Ⓐ Ⓑ Ⓒ Ⓓ Ⓔ	28. Ⓐ Ⓑ Ⓒ Ⓓ Ⓔ	48. Ⓐ Ⓑ Ⓒ Ⓓ Ⓔ
9. Ⓐ Ⓑ Ⓒ Ⓓ Ⓔ	29. Ⓐ Ⓑ Ⓒ Ⓓ Ⓔ	49. Ⓐ Ⓑ Ⓒ Ⓓ Ⓔ
10. Ⓐ Ⓑ Ⓒ Ⓓ Ⓔ	30. Ⓐ Ⓑ Ⓒ Ⓓ Ⓔ	50. Ⓐ Ⓑ Ⓒ Ⓓ Ⓔ
11. Ⓐ Ⓑ Ⓒ Ⓓ Ⓔ	31. Ⓐ Ⓑ Ⓒ Ⓓ Ⓔ	
12. Ⓐ Ⓑ Ⓒ Ⓓ Ⓔ	32. Ⓐ Ⓑ Ⓒ Ⓓ Ⓔ	
13. Ⓐ Ⓑ Ⓒ Ⓓ Ⓔ	33. Ⓐ Ⓑ Ⓒ Ⓓ Ⓔ	
14. Ⓐ Ⓑ Ⓒ Ⓓ Ⓔ	34. Ⓐ Ⓑ Ⓒ Ⓓ Ⓔ	
15. Ⓐ Ⓑ Ⓒ Ⓓ Ⓔ	35. Ⓐ Ⓑ Ⓒ Ⓓ Ⓔ	
16. Ⓐ Ⓑ Ⓒ Ⓓ Ⓔ	36. Ⓐ Ⓑ Ⓒ Ⓓ Ⓔ	
17. Ⓐ Ⓑ Ⓒ Ⓓ Ⓔ	37. Ⓐ Ⓑ Ⓒ Ⓓ Ⓔ	
18. Ⓐ Ⓑ Ⓒ Ⓓ Ⓔ	38. Ⓐ Ⓑ Ⓒ Ⓓ Ⓔ	
19. Ⓐ Ⓑ Ⓒ Ⓓ Ⓔ	39. Ⓐ Ⓑ Ⓒ Ⓓ Ⓔ	
20. Ⓐ Ⓑ Ⓒ Ⓓ Ⓔ	40. Ⓐ Ⓑ Ⓒ Ⓓ Ⓔ	

PRACTICE TEST 8

Time: 60 minutes

Directions: Select the BEST answer for each of the 50 multiple-choice questions. If the exact solution is not one of the five choices, select the answer that is the best approximation. Then, fill in the appropriate oval on the answer sheet.

Notes:

1. A calculator will be needed to answer some of the questions on the test. Scientific, programmable, and graphing calculators are permitted. It is up to you to determine when and when not to use your calculator.

2. Angles on the Level 2 test are measured in degrees and radians. You need to decide whether your calculator should be set to degree mode or radian mode for a particular question.

3. Figures are drawn as accurately as possible and are intended to help solve some of the test problems. If a figure is not drawn to scale, this will be stated in the problem. All figures lie in a plane unless the problem indicates otherwise.

4. Unless otherwise stated, the domain of a function f is assumed to be the set of real numbers x for which the value of the function, $f(x)$, is a real number.

5. Reference information that may be useful in answering some of the test questions can be found below.

Reference Information	
Right circular cone with radius r and height h:	Volume $= \dfrac{1}{3}\pi r^2 h$
Right circular cone with circumference of base c and slant height ℓ:	Lateral Area $= \dfrac{1}{2}c\ell$
Sphere with radius r:	Volume $= \dfrac{4}{3}\pi r^3$ Surface Area $= 4\pi r^2$
Pyramid with base area B and height h:	Volume $= \dfrac{1}{3}Bh$

PRACTICE TEST 8 QUESTIONS

1. $\dfrac{x^2 - x - 12}{2x^2 - 7x - 4} =$

   (A) $\dfrac{3(x-4)}{(x+4)}$

   (B) $\dfrac{2x-1}{x+4}$

   (C) $\dfrac{x+1}{x+4}$

   (D) $\dfrac{x+3}{2x+1}$

   (E) $\dfrac{2x-1}{x+1}$

2. $\sin^{-1}(\sin 200°) =$

   (A) $-20°$

   (B) $0°$

   (C) $20°$

   (D) $40°$

   (E) none of these

3. Soccer Supply Store has 24 soccer balls for sale. Sixteen of these cost \$12.99 and 8 cost \$19.99. If 2 soccer balls are selected at random, what is the probability that both have the lower price?

   (A) 0.43

   (B) 0.52

   (C) 0.65

   (D) 0.88

   (E) 0.96

4. The csc θ in the triangle below is equivalent to

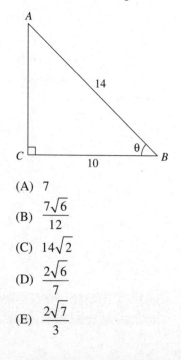

   (A) 7

   (B) $\dfrac{7\sqrt{6}}{12}$

   (C) $14\sqrt{2}$

   (D) $\dfrac{2\sqrt{6}}{7}$

   (E) $\dfrac{2\sqrt{7}}{3}$

GO ON TO THE NEXT PAGE

5. Nina puts $3000 into a bank account that pays 4% interest compounded annually. If she does not add any money, how much will she have in the account after 15 years?

   (A) $3075.00
   (B) $3120.00
   (C) $3509.58
   (D) $5402.83
   (E) $6200.26

6. $x^4 - x^3 =$

   (A) x^2
   (B) $x(1-x)$
   (C) $x^3(x-1)$
   (D) $\dfrac{x^4}{x^3}$
   (E) $2x^7$

7. If $f(x) = x + 5$, $g(x) = 2x - 2$, $h(x) = 2x$, $g(h(2x)) + f(x) = 18$, what is x?

   (A) 1
   (B) 3
   (C) 4
   (D) 7
   (E) 10

8. Five friends are getting on line to buy tickets for a concert. In how many different orders can they line up?

   (A) 20
   (B) 25
   (C) 32
   (D) 50
   (E) 120

9. A student rolls two dice. What is the probability that the sum will be greater than 8?

   (A) $\dfrac{3}{4}$

   (B) $\dfrac{8}{11}$

   (C) $\dfrac{5}{18}$

   (D) $\dfrac{5}{6}$

   (E) $\dfrac{1}{3}$

USE THIS SPACE AS SCRATCH PAPER

GO ON TO THE NEXT PAGE

10. What is the distance between the lines $2y - 6x = -2$ and $-3x + y = 2$?

    (A) 0.23
    (B) 0.55
    (C) 1.32
    (D) 1.85
    (E) 3.60

11. If a circle has a radius of 8, the area of a sector with a central angle of 40° to the nearest whole number is

    (A) 11
    (B) 22
    (C) 28
    (D) 48
    (E) 53

12. Which of the following is equivalent to $\log_a 3 + \log_a x - \log_a 2$?

    (A) $\log_a \left(\dfrac{2x}{3} \right)$

    (B) $\log_a \left(\dfrac{3x}{2} \right)$

    (C) $\dfrac{3}{2} \log_a x$

    (D) $3 \log_a \dfrac{2x}{2}$

    (E) $2 \log_a 3x$

13. What is the domain of $f(x) = \dfrac{3\sqrt{x+2}}{x-1}$?

    (A) $\{x: x \geq -2 \text{ and } x \neq 1\}$
    (B) $\{x: x \geq -1 \text{ and } x \neq -2\}$
    (C) $\{x: x \geq 0\}$
    (D) $\{x: x \geq -\dfrac{1}{2}\}$
    (E) all real numbers

14. What are the coordinates of the vertex of the parabola whose equation is $4x^2 - 8x + 2$?

    (A) (1, 2)
    (B) (2, −1)
    (C) (2, −8)
    (D) (−8, 2)
    (E) (1, −2)

15. If $f(x) = 2\sqrt{3x}$, what is the value of $f^{-1}(6)$?

    (A) 3
    (B) 6
    (C) 9
    (D) 12
    (E) 16

GO ON TO THE NEXT PAGE

16. Which of the following is parallel to the line $4y - x = 12$?

(A) $y = 4x + 6$

(B) $y = \dfrac{1}{4}x - 2$

(C) $y = -4x + 4$

(D) $y = \dfrac{1}{2}x + 12$

(E) $y = 12x - 4$

17. Which set of data values has the greatest range?

(A) $\{62, 63, 64, 65\}$
(B) $\{3, 6, 9, 12\}$
(C) $\{2, 4, 6, 8\}$
(D) $\{15, 15, 15, 15\}$
(E) $\{40, 50, 60, 70\}$

18. The 6th term of an arithmetic sequence is -10 and the common difference is -5. What is the first term of the sequence?

(A) -10
(B) -5
(C) 0
(D) 10
(E) 15

19. If $\sin \theta = \dfrac{4}{5}$ and $\cos \theta = \dfrac{3}{5}$, what is $\sin 2\theta$?

(A) $\dfrac{8}{5}$

(B) $\dfrac{24}{25}$

(C) $\dfrac{12}{25}$

(D) $\dfrac{12}{5}$

(E) $\dfrac{5}{7}$

20. Which of the following lines are vertical asymptotes of the graph of $y = \dfrac{2x+4}{x^2+5x+6}$?

    I. $x = -2$
    II. $x = 0$
    III. $x = -3$

(A) I only
(B) II only
(C) III only
(D) I and III
(E) II and III

USE THIS SPACE AS SCRATCH PAPER

GO ON TO THE NEXT PAGE

21. The graph below represents

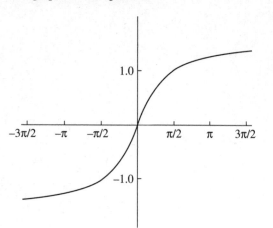

(A) $\sin^{-1}$
(B) $\cos^{-1}$
(C) $\tan^{-1}$
(D) $\csc^{-1}$
(E) $\sec^{-1}$

22. Which is an endpoint of the major axis of the ellipse whose equation is $x^2 + 5y^2 = 5$?

(A) $(0, 1)$

(B) $(\sqrt{5}, 0)$

(C) $(-1, 0)$

(D) $(\sqrt{5}, 1)$

(E) $(1, \sqrt{5})$

23. If $x = 4 + 2i$, $x^2 =$

(A) $2 - 12i$
(B) $16 + 12i$
(C) $8 + 6i$
(D) $-1 + 6i$
(E) $12 + 16i$

24. Convert 45° to radians.

(A) $\dfrac{\pi}{4}$

(B) $\dfrac{\pi}{2}$

(C) $\dfrac{3\pi}{2}$

(D) $\dfrac{2\pi}{3}$

(E) 4π

GO ON TO THE NEXT PAGE

25. Which of the following functions transforms $y = f(x)$ by moving it 6 units downward?

    (A) $y = f(x + 6)$
    (B) $y = f(x - 6)$
    (C) $y = f(x) + 6$
    (D) $y = f(x) - 6$
    (E) $y = \dfrac{1}{6} f(x)$

26. To the nearest 10th, the positive zero of $y = 2x^2 - 6x - 3$ is

    (A) 0.4
    (B) 0.6
    (C) 1.8
    (D) 2.9
    (E) 3.4

27. The y-intercept of the line that passes through the points $(-1, 10)$ and $(2, -8)$ is

    (A) -6
    (B) -3
    (C) 3
    (D) 4
    (E) 12

28. How can $\left(\dfrac{a^2 b^{-4}}{c^{-3} d^5}\right)^6 =$ be expressed with only positive exponents?

    (A) $\dfrac{c^{18} d^{30}}{a^{12} b^{24}}$

    (B) $\dfrac{a^{12} b^{24}}{c^{18} d^{30}}$

    (C) $\dfrac{c^9 d^{15}}{a^6 b^{12}}$

    (D) $\dfrac{a^{12} c^{18}}{b^{24} d^{30}}$

    (E) $\dfrac{6a^2 b^4}{6c^3 d^5}$

29. If $f(x) = \sqrt{x} - 4$, then $f^{-1}(x)$ is

    (A) $x^2 + 8x + 16$
    (B) $x^2 + 16$
    (C) $x^2 + 4$
    (D) $x - 2$
    (E) $4x + 1$

GO ON TO THE NEXT PAGE

30. What are the coordinates of the vertex of the parabola whose equation is $y = x^2 - 2x + 2$?

    (A) $(1, -2)$
    (B) $(-1, 2)$
    (C) $(1, 1)$
    (D) $(-1, -2)$
    (E) $(2, -1)$

31. If $4x + 3y = 26$ and $3x + 4y = 30$, what is $x - y$?

    (A) -4
    (B) -2
    (C) 0
    (D) 2
    (E) 6

32. If $x - 3$ is a factor of $x^3 - x^2 - kx + 3$, what is the value of k?

    (A) -3
    (B) -1
    (C) 3
    (D) 6
    (E) 7

33. A black bag contains 10 beads, 3 of which are gold. A white bag contains 6 beads, 2 of which are gold. If a bead is drawn at random from each bag, what is the probability that one bead is gold and one is not?

    (A) $\dfrac{1}{3}$

    (B) $\dfrac{9}{16}$

    (C) $\dfrac{6}{7}$

    (D) $\dfrac{7}{10}$

    (E) $\dfrac{13}{30}$

34. If $f(x) = \sqrt{x}$ and $g(x) = 2x^2$, $(f \circ g)(x)$ equals

    (A) $\sqrt{2x}$

    (B) $\sqrt{2 - x^2}$

    (C) $\dfrac{x^2}{2}$

    (D) $2\sqrt{x}$

    (E) $x\sqrt{2}$

USE THIS SPACE AS SCRATCH PAPER

GO ON TO THE NEXT PAGE

35. What is the smallest distance between point $(1, 7)$ and a point on the circumference of the circle described by $(x + 2)^2 + (y - 3)^2 = 49$?

    (A) 1
    (B) 2
    (C) 3
    (D) 4
    (E) 5

36. The slope of the linear function, f, is 4. If $f(-1) = -10$ and $f(2) = z$, what is z?

    (A) -6
    (B) $-\dfrac{1}{2}$
    (C) 2
    (D) $\dfrac{3}{2}$
    (E) 12

37. What is the equation of a sphere that has a diameter extending from $(1, 3, -5)$ to $(3, -1, 3)$?

    (A) $(x + 3)^2 + (y - 1)^2 + (z + 3)^2 = 4$
    (B) $(x - 1)^2 + (y - 3)^2 + (z + 5)^2 = 16$
    (C) $(x - 2)^2 + (y - 3)^2 + (z + 5)^2 = 18$
    (D) $(x + 2)^2 + (y + 1)^2 + (z + 1)^2 = 21$
    (E) $(x - 2)^2 + (y - 1)^2 + (z + 1)^2 = 21$

38. Which is the modulus of $18 + 24i$?

    (A) $\sqrt{6}$
    (B) $\sqrt{42}$
    (C) 25
    (D) 30
    (E) 42

39. Records at an animal kennel one weekend show that 70% of the animals are dogs and 35% of the dogs are Labradors. If an animal is selected at random, what is the probability that the animal is a Labrador dog?

    (A) 0.25
    (B) 0.30
    (C) 0.35
    (D) 0.40
    (E) 0.50

40. $\log_2 14 =$

    (A) 0.26
    (B) 0.35
    (C) 3.20
    (D) 3.81
    (E) 4.03

USE THIS SPACE AS SCRATCH PAPER

GO ON TO THE NEXT PAGE

41. The area of the triangle shown is
    (A) 30.0
    (B) 43.3
    (C) 48.5
    (D) 51.9
    (E) 96.9

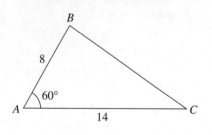

42. If point $P(8, 15)$ lies on the terminal side of $\angle\theta$ in standard position, $\cos\theta =$

    (A) $\dfrac{8}{15}$

    (B) $\dfrac{17}{8}$

    (C) $\dfrac{15}{8}$

    (D) $\dfrac{15}{17}$

    (E) $\dfrac{8}{17}$

43. What is the domain of $f(x) = \dfrac{3}{x+5}$?

    (A) $\{x: x \neq -5\}$
    (B) $\{x: x \geq 0\}$
    (C) $\{x: x < -3\}$
    (D) $\{x: x > -5\}$
    (E) all real numbers

44. What is the perimeter of the isosceles triangle below?

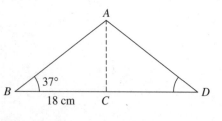

    (A) 22.5 cm
    (B) 44.7 cm
    (C) 58.5 cm
    (D) 79.9 cm
    (E) 81.1 cm

GO ON TO THE NEXT PAGE

45. Which equation describes the graph?

   (A) $y = x + 2$

   (B) $y = \dfrac{x^2 - 4}{x + 2}$

   (C) $y = x^2 - 4$

   (D) $y = 2x + 4$

   (E) $y = x^2$

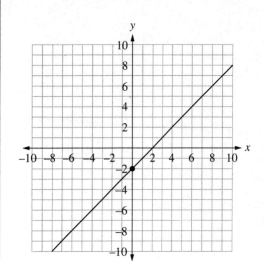

46. If $f(x) = 3x + 2$, what value of x makes $f(f(x)) = -10$?

   (A) -2

   (B) -1

   (C) $\dfrac{1}{2}$

   (D) 8

   (E) 12

47. If the graph of $f^{-1}(x)$ is as shown, $f(x)$ is

   (A) x

   (B) $\dfrac{1}{x}$

   (C) $\sqrt{x}$

   (D) x^2

   (E) $2x + 1$

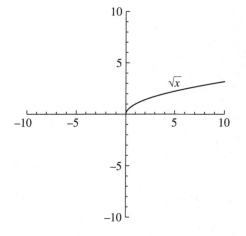

GO ON TO THE NEXT PAGE

48. Which equation describes the graph?

(A) $\dfrac{x^2}{5} + \dfrac{y^2}{4} = 1$

(B) $\dfrac{x^2}{10} + \dfrac{y^2}{8} = 1$

(C) $\dfrac{x^2}{25} + \dfrac{y^2}{16} = 1$

(D) $\dfrac{x^2}{4} + \dfrac{y^2}{1} = 1$

(E) $x^2 + y^2 = 20$

USE THIS SPACE AS SCRATCH PAPER

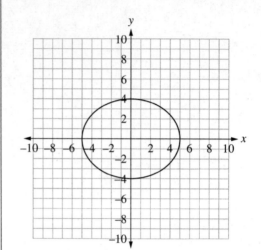

49. Which is the product of $(4 + 4i)(2 + 2i)$ in standard form?

(A) $16i$
(B) $8 + 8i$
(C) $6 + 2i$
(D) $2 + 4i$
(E) $8i$

50. The period of $f(x) = 2\sin\left(3x - \dfrac{\pi}{2}\right)$ is

(A) $\dfrac{2}{3}$

(B) $\dfrac{2\pi}{3}$

(C) $\dfrac{\pi}{2}$

(D) $\dfrac{3\pi}{2}$

(E) 2

S T O P

IF YOU FINISH BEFORE TIME IS CALLED, YOU MAY CHECK YOUR WORK ON THIS TEST ONLY.
DO NOT TURN TO ANY OTHER TEST IN THIS BOOK.

ANSWER KEY

1. D	11. B	21. C	31. A	41. C
2. A	12. B	22. B	32. E	42. E
3. A	13. A	23. E	33. E	43. A
4. B	14. E	24. A	34. E	44. E
5. D	15. D	25. D	35. B	45. A
6. C	16. B	26. E	36. C	46. A
7. B	17. E	27. D	37. E	47. D
8. E	18. E	28. D	38. D	48. C
9. C	19. B	29. A	39. A	49. A
10. B	20. C	30. C	40. D	50. B

ANSWERS AND EXPLANATIONS

1. **(D)** Factor the numerator and denominator to get: $\dfrac{x+3(x-4)}{2x+1(x-4)}$. Cancel $(x-4)$.

2. **(A)** Enter 2nd sin sin 200° into your calculator set to degrees.

3. **(A)** The probability that the first ball selected has the lower price is $\dfrac{16}{24}$. Once it is selected, there are 23 balls remaining. The probability that the second ball selected also has the lower price is $\dfrac{15}{23}$. The probability that both balls have the lower price is $\dfrac{16}{24} \cdot \dfrac{15}{23} \approx 0.43$.

4. **(B)** First, find AC: $(AC)^2 + 10^2 = 14^2$, so $AC = \sqrt{96} = 4\sqrt{6}$. Then $\csc \theta = \dfrac{AB}{AC} = \dfrac{14}{4\sqrt{6}} = \dfrac{7\sqrt{6}}{12}$.

5. **(D)** Find $3000 \cdot 1.04^{15} = \$5402.83$.

6. **(C)** Factor out the greatest common factor, which is x^3. Therefore, $x^4 - x^3 = x^3(x-1)$.

7. **(B)** $g(h(2)) - f(x) = 18$ so $g(4x) + (x+2) = 18$, which becomes $2(4x) - 2 + (x+2) = 18$. Therefore, $4x - 2 + x + 5 = 18$ so $5x = 15$ and $x = 3$.

8. **(E)** The number of possible ways the friends can line up is 5!, which equals 120.

9. **(C)** There are 36 elements in the sample space. Of those, 10 elements are greater than 8. Therefore, the probability is $\dfrac{10}{36}$ or $\dfrac{5}{18}$.

10. **(B)** Rewrite the equations in simplest form. They become $-3x + y + 1 = 0$ and $-3x + y - 2 = 0$. The lines are parallel, so use the equation $d = \dfrac{|C_1 - C_2|}{\sqrt{A^2 + B^2}}$. Therefore, $d = \dfrac{|1 - (-2)|}{\sqrt{(-3)^2 + 2^2}}$, which becomes $\dfrac{2}{\sqrt{13}}$, or 0.55.

11. **(B)** $A = \left(\dfrac{\theta}{360}\right)\pi r^2 = \left(\dfrac{40}{360}\right)\pi 8^2 \approx 22.3$.

An alternate method is to determine that the sector is $\dfrac{1}{9}$ of the total area of the circle. Therefore, calculating the area and finding $\dfrac{1}{9}$ will provide the same result.

12. **(B)** Use the properties of logarithms: $\log_a 3 + \log_a x - \log_a 2 = \log_a(3x) - \log_a 2$, which becomes $\log_a\left(\dfrac{3x}{2}\right)$.

13. **(A)** There are two limitations on this function. The radicand cannot be negative. Therefore, the quantity $x + 2$ must be greater than or equal to zero, $x \geq -2$. The denominator cannot be zero. Therefore, x cannot be equal to 1.

14. **(E)** The x-coordinate is $-\dfrac{b}{2a} = -\dfrac{(-8)}{8} = 1$. The y-coordinate is $4(1)^2 - 8(1) + 2 = -2$. Therefore the vertex occurs at the point $(1, -2)$.

15. **(D)** $f^{-1}(6)$ is the value of x that makes $2\sqrt{3x}$ equal to 6. To find x, set $2\sqrt{3x} = 6$ and divide both sides by 2 to get $\sqrt{3x} = 3$, so $x = 3$.

16. **(B)** Rewrite the equation in the form $y = \dfrac{1}{4}x + 3$. The slope of the given line is $\dfrac{1}{4}$. The slope of the line that is parallel is the same. Only choice B has a slope of $\dfrac{1}{4}$.

17. **(E)** The range is the spread of the data. To find the range of each set, subtract the lowest value from the greatest value.

18. **(E)** $a_n = a_1 + (n-1)d$, so $-10 = a_1 + (6-1) - 5$, and $a_1 = 15$.

19. **(B)** Use the double angle formula: $\sin 2\theta = 2(\sin \theta)(\cos \theta) = 2\left(\dfrac{4}{5}\right)\left(\dfrac{3}{5}\right) = \dfrac{24}{25}$, or, find θ by using inverse sin, then double the answer and calculate.

20. **(C)** The vertical asymptotes are the nonremovable values of x that make the denominator zero. Set the denominator equal to zero and solve. $x^2 + 5x + 6 = 0$. $(x + 2)$ cancels with the numerator, so that leaves $(x + 3)$. Therefore, $x = -3$.

21. **(C)** An inverse function is reflected about the line $y = x$. The only function that is the reflection represented is the inverse tangent.

22. **(B)** Write the equation in standard form by dividing both sides of the equation by 5 to get $\dfrac{x^2}{5} + \dfrac{y^2}{1} = 1$. Therefore, $a = \sqrt{5}$ and $b = 1$. The endpoints of the major axis are $(\sqrt{5}, 0)$ and $(-\sqrt{5}, 0)$.

23. **(E)** Enter the expression into your graphing calculator. An alternate method is to perform the multiplication using the foil method, remembering that $i^2 = -1$.

$(4 + 2i)(4 + 2i)$
$16 + 8i + 8i + 4i^2$
$16 + 16i - 4$
$12 + 16i$

24. **(A)** Convert from degrees to radians: $45°\left(\dfrac{\pi^R}{180°}\right) = \dfrac{\pi^R}{4}$.

25. **(D)** The function $g(x)$ is translated as $g(x) + k$ downward if $k < 0$, and upward if $k > 0$.

26. **(E)** Enter the values into the quadratic formula program on your graphing calculator, or test answers in function. Choose the positive zero and round to the nearest 10th.

27. **(D)** The slope of the line is $\dfrac{10 - (-8)}{-1 - 2} = \dfrac{18}{-3} = -6$. The point-slope equation is then $y - 10 = -6(x + 1)$. Solve for y to get $y = -6x + 4$. The y-intercept of the line is 4.

28. **(D)** Apply the exponent: $\left(\dfrac{a^2b^{-4}}{c^{-3}d^5}\right)^6 = \dfrac{a^{12}b^{-24}}{c^{-18}d^{30}}$. Then rewrite as: $\dfrac{a^{12}c^{18}}{b^{24}d^{30}}$.

29. **(A)** Replace $f(x)$ with y. $f(x) = \sqrt{x} - 4$ becomes $y = \sqrt{x} - 4$. Then interchange x and y: $x = \sqrt{y} - 4$. Solve for y: $x + 4 = \sqrt{y}$; $(x + 4)^2 = y$; $y = x^2 + 8x + 16$.

30. **(C)** The x-coordinate is $x = -\dfrac{b}{2a} = -\dfrac{-2}{2} = 1$. The y-coordinate is $y = (1)^2 - 2(1) + 2 = 1$. Therefore, the vertex occurs at the point $(1, 1)$.

31. **(A)** Subtract the equations: $(4x + 3y) - (3x + 4y) = 26 - 30$, which becomes $x - y = -4$.

32. **(E)** If $x - 3$ is a factor, it should divide into the polynomial without a remainder. Use synthetic division to solve:

3	1	−1	−k	3
		3	6	−3k + 18
	2	−k + 6	−3k + 21	

Set the remainder equal to 0 and solve for k: $-3k + 21 = 0$, so $k = 7$.

33. (E) The probability that the bead from the black bag is gold and the bead from the white bag is not is $\frac{3}{10} \cdot \frac{4}{6} = \frac{12}{60}$. The probability that the bead from the black bag is not gold and the bead from the white bag is gold is $\frac{7}{10} \cdot \frac{2}{6} = \frac{14}{60}$. Because these events are mutually exclusive, add the probabilities together: $\frac{12}{60} + \frac{14}{60} = \frac{26}{60} = \frac{13}{30}$.

34. (E) $(f \circ g)(x) = f(g(x))$ so $f(2x^2) = \sqrt{2x^2} = x\sqrt{2}$.

35. (B) Use the equation to find that the center of the circle is at $(-2, 3)$ and the radius is 7. Then use the distance formula to find the distance from the center to point $(1, 7)$. $d = \sqrt{(-2-1)^2 + (3-7)^2} = 5$. Finally, subtract the radius of the circle from the distance to the given point.

36. (C) The line goes through the points $(-1, -10)$ and $(2, z)$. Use the formula to find the slope and then use the given slope to solve for b: $m = \frac{z-(-10)}{2-(-1)} = \frac{z+10}{3}$ and $\frac{z+10}{3} = 4$, so $z = 2$.

37. (E) Use the midpoint formula to find the center of the sphere: $\left(\frac{1+3}{2}, \frac{3+(-1)}{2}, \frac{-5+3}{2}\right) = (2, 1, -1)$. Use the distance formula to calculate the radius: $r = \frac{1}{2}\sqrt{(3-1)^2 + (-1-3)^2 + (3-(-5))^2} = \frac{1}{2}\sqrt{84} = \frac{1}{2}(2)\sqrt{21} = \sqrt{21}$. Then use the results to describe the equation: $(x-2)^2 + (y-1)^2 + (z+1)^2 = 21$.

38. (D) The real and imaginary parts of the complex number are 18 and 24. Therefore, the modulus is $\sqrt{18^2 + 24^2} = \sqrt{900} = 30$.

39. (A) The probability that the animal at the kennel is a dog is 0.7. The probability that the dog is a Labrador is 0.35. The probability that the animal is a Labrador dog is $(0.7)(0.35) = 0.245$, or about 0.25.

40. (D) Use the change-of-base formula to find $\frac{\log 14}{\log 2}$ by entering the values on your calculator.

41. (C) $A = \frac{1}{2}ab \cdot \sin A = \frac{1}{2}(8)(14)(0.866) \approx 48.5$.

42. (E) It is most useful to draw a diagram to solve the problem.

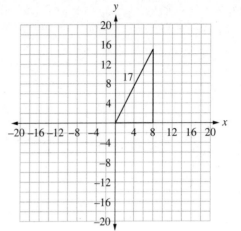

Use the Pythagorean Theorem to calculate the length of the hypotenuse as 17. Therefore, $\cos \theta = \frac{8}{17}$.

43. (A) Determine the values of x that would make the denominator zero. $x + 5 = 0$ so $x = -5$.

44. (E) The altitude bisects the triangle to form two, congruent right triangles. Determine the length of AB. $\cos 37° = \frac{18}{AB}$, so $AB = \frac{18}{\cos 37°} = 22.54$. Therefore, the perimeter equals $22.54 + 22.54 + 36 = 81.1$ cm.

45. (A) There is a discontinuity at $x = -2$. Therefore, the graph represents a function that is undefined at this value. The value must either make the denominator of a fraction 0 or the radicand of a square root negative.

46. (A) $f(f(x)) = 3(3x + 2) + 2 = 9x + 6 + 2 = 9x + 8$. Set this equal to -10 and solve for x. $9x + 8 = -10$, and $x = -2$.

47. (D) The graph shows a square root function, which is the inverse of a parabola. The equation for a parabola includes a square.

48. (C) The major axis is 10, so $a = 5$. The minor axis is 8 so $b = 4$. Insert these values into the standard equation for an ellipse $\frac{x^2}{a^2} + \frac{y^2}{b^2} = 1$.

49. (A) The fastest method is to enter the problem into your calculator. Use 2nd decimal to enter i. Alternatively, you can use the foil method to multiply and remember to replace i^2 with -1.

50. (B) When $f(x)$ is in the form $a \sin(bx + c)$, the period is $\frac{2\pi}{|b|} = \frac{2\pi}{3}$.

▒▒▒▒ DIAGNOSE YOUR STRENGTHS AND WEAKNESSES

Check the number of each question answered correctly and "X" the number of each question answered incorrectly.

Algebra and Functions	1	5	6	7	10	12	13	14	15	16	20	26	27	Total Number Correct
25 questions														
	28	29	30	31	32	34	36	40	43	45	46	47		

Trigonometry	2	4	11	19	21	24	42	44	50	Total Number Correct
9 questions										

Coordinate and Three-Dimensional Geometry	22	25	35	37	41	48	Total Number Correct
6 questions							

Numbers and Operations	8	18	23	38	49	Total Number Correct
5 questions						

Data Analysis, Statistics, and Probability	3	9	17	33	39	Total Number Correct
5 questions						

Number of correct answers $-\dfrac{1}{4}$ **(Number of incorrect answers) = Your raw score**

_____ $-\dfrac{1}{4}$ (_____) = _____

Compare your raw score with the approximate SAT Subject Test score below:

	Raw Score	SAT Subject Test Approximate Score
Excellent	43–50	770–800
Very Good	33–43	670–770
Good	27–33	620–670
Above Average	21–27	570–620
Average	11–21	500–570
Below Average	< 11	< 500

PRACTICE TEST 9

Treat this practice test as the actual test and complete it in one 60-minute sitting. Use the following answer sheet to fill in your multiple-choice answers. Once you have completed the practice test:

1. Check your answers using the Answer Key.
2. Review the Answers and Solutions.
3. Fill in the "Diagnose Your Strengths and Weaknesses" sheet, and determine areas that require further preparation.

PRACTICE TEST 9

MATH LEVEL 2

ANSWER SHEET

Tear out this answer sheet and use it to complete the practice test. Determine the BEST answer for each question. Then, fill in the appropriate oval using a No. 2 pencil.

1. Ⓐ Ⓑ Ⓒ Ⓓ Ⓔ	21. Ⓐ Ⓑ Ⓒ Ⓓ Ⓔ	41. Ⓐ Ⓑ Ⓒ Ⓓ Ⓔ
2. Ⓐ Ⓑ Ⓒ Ⓓ Ⓔ	22. Ⓐ Ⓑ Ⓒ Ⓓ Ⓔ	42. Ⓐ Ⓑ Ⓒ Ⓓ Ⓔ
3. Ⓐ Ⓑ Ⓒ Ⓓ Ⓔ	23. Ⓐ Ⓑ Ⓒ Ⓓ Ⓔ	43. Ⓐ Ⓑ Ⓒ Ⓓ Ⓔ
4. Ⓐ Ⓑ Ⓒ Ⓓ Ⓔ	24. Ⓐ Ⓑ Ⓒ Ⓓ Ⓔ	44. Ⓐ Ⓑ Ⓒ Ⓓ Ⓔ
5. Ⓐ Ⓑ Ⓒ Ⓓ Ⓔ	25. Ⓐ Ⓑ Ⓒ Ⓓ Ⓔ	45. Ⓐ Ⓑ Ⓒ Ⓓ Ⓔ
6. Ⓐ Ⓑ Ⓒ Ⓓ Ⓔ	26. Ⓐ Ⓑ Ⓒ Ⓓ Ⓔ	46. Ⓐ Ⓑ Ⓒ Ⓓ Ⓔ
7. Ⓐ Ⓑ Ⓒ Ⓓ Ⓔ	27. Ⓐ Ⓑ Ⓒ Ⓓ Ⓔ	47. Ⓐ Ⓑ Ⓒ Ⓓ Ⓔ
8. Ⓐ Ⓑ Ⓒ Ⓓ Ⓔ	28. Ⓐ Ⓑ Ⓒ Ⓓ Ⓔ	48. Ⓐ Ⓑ Ⓒ Ⓓ Ⓔ
9. Ⓐ Ⓑ Ⓒ Ⓓ Ⓔ	29. Ⓐ Ⓑ Ⓒ Ⓓ Ⓔ	49. Ⓐ Ⓑ Ⓒ Ⓓ Ⓔ
10. Ⓐ Ⓑ Ⓒ Ⓓ Ⓔ	30. Ⓐ Ⓑ Ⓒ Ⓓ Ⓔ	50. Ⓐ Ⓑ Ⓒ Ⓓ Ⓔ
11. Ⓐ Ⓑ Ⓒ Ⓓ Ⓔ	31. Ⓐ Ⓑ Ⓒ Ⓓ Ⓔ	
12. Ⓐ Ⓑ Ⓒ Ⓓ Ⓔ	32. Ⓐ Ⓑ Ⓒ Ⓓ Ⓔ	
13. Ⓐ Ⓑ Ⓒ Ⓓ Ⓔ	33. Ⓐ Ⓑ Ⓒ Ⓓ Ⓔ	
14. Ⓐ Ⓑ Ⓒ Ⓓ Ⓔ	34. Ⓐ Ⓑ Ⓒ Ⓓ Ⓔ	
15. Ⓐ Ⓑ Ⓒ Ⓓ Ⓔ	35. Ⓐ Ⓑ Ⓒ Ⓓ Ⓔ	
16. Ⓐ Ⓑ Ⓒ Ⓓ Ⓔ	36. Ⓐ Ⓑ Ⓒ Ⓓ Ⓔ	
17. Ⓐ Ⓑ Ⓒ Ⓓ Ⓔ	37. Ⓐ Ⓑ Ⓒ Ⓓ Ⓔ	
18. Ⓐ Ⓑ Ⓒ Ⓓ Ⓔ	38. Ⓐ Ⓑ Ⓒ Ⓓ Ⓔ	
19. Ⓐ Ⓑ Ⓒ Ⓓ Ⓔ	39. Ⓐ Ⓑ Ⓒ Ⓓ Ⓔ	
20. Ⓐ Ⓑ Ⓒ Ⓓ Ⓔ	40. Ⓐ Ⓑ Ⓒ Ⓓ Ⓔ	

PRACTICE TEST 9

Time: 60 minutes

Directions: Select the BEST answer for each of the 50 multiple-choice questions. If the exact solution is not one of the five choices, select the answer that is the best approximation. Then, fill in the appropriate oval on the answer sheet.

Notes:

1. A calculator will be needed to answer some of the questions on the test. Scientific, programmable, and graphing calculators are permitted. It is up to you to determine when and when not to use your calculator.
2. Angles on the Level 2 test are measured in degrees and radians. You need to decide whether your calculator should be set to degree mode or radian mode for a particular question.
3. Figures are drawn as accurately as possible and are intended to help solve some of the test problems. If a figure is not drawn to scale, this will be stated in the problem. All figures lie in a plane unless the problem indicates otherwise.
4. Unless otherwise stated, the domain of a function f is assumed to be the set of real numbers x for which the value of the function, $f(x)$, is a real number.
5. Reference information that may be useful in answering some of the test questions can be found below.

Reference Information	
Right circular cone with radius r and height h:	Volume $= \dfrac{1}{3}\pi r^2 h$
Right circular cone with circumference of base c and slant height ℓ:	Lateral Area $= \dfrac{1}{2} c\ell$
Sphere with radius r:	Volume $= \dfrac{4}{3}\pi r^3$ Surface Area $= 4\pi r^2$
Pyramid with base area B and height h:	Volume $= \dfrac{1}{3} Bh$

PRACTICE TEST 9 QUESTIONS

1. Which one of the following must be removed if {(2, 5), (4, 6), (5, 9), (8, 11), (4, 13)} is to be a function?

   (A) (5, 9)
   (B) (8, 11)
   (C) (4, 13)
   (D) (2, 5)
   (E) none of these

USE THIS SPACE AS SCRATCH PAPER

2. Which polar coordinates can be used to describe the point shown?

   (A) (7, 48.59°)
   (B) (9, 13.09°)
   (C) (10, 36.87°)
   (D) (13, 10°)
   (E) (10, 53.13°)

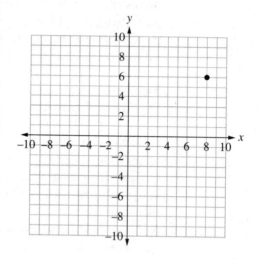

3. If $f(x) = x^2 + 3x - 1, f(-3) =$

   (A) −1
   (B) 0
   (C) 1
   (D) 9
   (E) 17

4. If $f(x) = 8x + 2$, then $f^{-1}(x)$ could be represented by

   (A) $2x - 4$
   (B) $\dfrac{x-2}{8}$
   (C) $\dfrac{2x}{3}$
   (D) $\dfrac{x}{8}$
   (E) $\dfrac{x+2}{2}$

5. The range of the function $f = \{(x, y): 6 - 2x - x^2\}$ is

   (A) $\{y: y \geq -7\}$
   (B) $\{y: y \leq 0\}$
   (C) $\{y: y \leq 6\}$
   (D) $\{y: y \leq 7\}$
   (E) $\{y: y \leq 0\}$

GO ON TO THE NEXT PAGE

6. If a circle has a radius of 12 inches, the area of a sector with a central angle of 2.5 radians to the nearest whole number is

(A) 58
(B) 72
(C) 90
(D) 144
(E) 180

7. The 10th term of the sequence 5, 15, 45, 135, ...

(A) 5000
(B) 7290
(C) 19,683
(D) 98,415
(E) 105,125

8. The sum of the zeros of $f(x) = 5x^2 - 2$ is

(A) 2.2
(B) 1.7
(C) 1.4
(D) 0.8
(E) 0

9. If $\sqrt{k} = 4.243$, then $\sqrt{10k} =$

(A) 6.5
(B) 13.4
(C) 42.4
(D) 179.6
(E) 4243

10. If $5x + 3y = 34$ and $4x + 4y = 32$, what is $x - y$?

(A) −4
(B) −2
(C) 0
(D) 2
(E) 6

11. A ladder leans against a building as shown. How long is the ladder?

(A) $\dfrac{\sqrt{2}}{11}$ ft

(B) 11 ft

(C) $11\sqrt{2}$ ft

(D) 16.5 ft

(E) $22\sqrt{2}$ ft

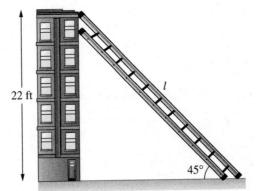

GO ON TO THE NEXT PAGE

12. If $f(x) = x^2 + 2x$, then $f(2b + 1) =$
    (A) $4b^2 + 4b + 1$
    (B) $4b^2 + 8b + 3$
    (C) $2b^2 + 2b + 4$
    (D) $b^2 + 12b + 8$
    (E) $b^2 + 8b + 1$

13. If x, y, and z are positive, and $xy = 20$, $xz = 30$, and $yz = 24$, then $xyz =$
    (A) 15
    (B) 30
    (C) 80
    (D) 120
    (E) 160

14. $\left| 9^{-\frac{1}{2}} - 2(12^0) \right|$

    (A) 1
    (B) $\dfrac{1}{9}$
    (C) $\dfrac{5}{3}$
    (D) 2
    (E) 6

15. Which is the equation of a circle that has a diameter with endpoints at $A(0, 3)$ and $B(4, 3)$?
    (A) $(x - 0)^2 + (y - 3)^2 = 4$
    (B) $(x + 2)^2 + (y - 1)^2 = 9$
    (C) $(x - 3)^2 + (y - 2)^2 = 4$
    (D) $(x + 3)^2 + (y + 2)^2 = 2$
    (E) $(x - 2)^2 + (y - 3)^2 = 4$

16. Which of the following is parallel to the line $y - 3x = 4$?
    (A) $y = 4x + 3$
    (B) $y = -\dfrac{1}{3}x + 4$
    (C) $y = -3x - 1$
    (D) $y = \dfrac{1}{3}x + 3$
    (E) $y = 3x - 4$

17. If $2 \log_6 x = \log_6 9$, what is the value of x?
    (A) 2
    (B) 3
    (C) 6
    (D) 9
    (E) 18

USE THIS SPACE AS SCRATCH PAPER

GO ON TO THE NEXT PAGE

18. A student rolls 2 dice. What is the probability that the sum will be equal to 9?

    (A) $\dfrac{3}{4}$

    (B) $\dfrac{1}{3}$

    (C) $\dfrac{1}{18}$

    (D) $\dfrac{5}{6}$

    (E) $\dfrac{1}{9}$

19. What is the sum of the roots of $y = 2x^2 + 6x - 8$?

    (A) −10
    (B) −3
    (C) −1
    (D) 4
    (E) 6

20. Which point is a focus of the ellipse whose equation is $\dfrac{x^2}{25} + \dfrac{y^2}{36} = 1$?

    (A) $(0, 6)$
    (B) $(5, \sqrt{11})$
    (C) $(0, -6)$
    (D) $(\sqrt{11}, 6)$
    (E) $(0, -\sqrt{11})$

21. $\cos(\cos^{-1} 0.86) =$

    (A) 0.07
    (B) 0.86
    (C) 7.8
    (D) 12
    (E) 31

22. Which of the following functions stretches $y = \cos(x)$ vertically by a factor of 2?

    (A) $y = 2\cos(x)$
    (B) $y = \cos(x + 2)$
    (C) $y = \cos(2x)$
    (D) $y = \cos(x) + 2$
    (E) $y = \dfrac{1}{2}\cos(x)$

23. $\dfrac{\pi}{6}$ radians is equivalent to

    (A) 16°
    (B) 22.5°
    (C) 30°
    (D) 45°
    (E) 60°

USE THIS SPACE AS SCRATCH PAPER

GO ON TO THE NEXT PAGE

24. If x is a complex number shown on the graph, which
     point could be ix?

     (A) A
     (B) B
     (C) C
     (D) D
     (E) E

USE THIS SPACE AS SCRATCH PAPER

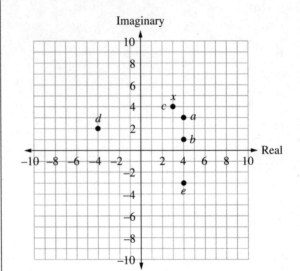

25. What is the domain of $f(x) = \dfrac{x+2}{x^2+x-6}$?

     (A) $\{x: x \neq -3 \text{ or } 2\}$
     (B) $\{x: x \geq 0\}$
     (C) $\{x: x < -3\}$
     (D) $\{x: x > 2\}$
     (E) all real numbers

26. To the nearest tenth, the positive zero of $y = x^2 + 4x - 2$
     is

     (A) 0.4
     (B) 0.6
     (C) 1.5
     (D) 3.8
     (E) 4.4

27. A bowler scored 180, 152, 165, 170, and 205 in
     5 games. What must the player bowl next to have an
     average of 175?

     (A) 165
     (B) 174
     (C) 178
     (D) 182
     (E) 210

28. If $x + 4$ is a factor of $2x^3 + 11x^2 + kx - 8$, what is the
     value of k?

     (A) -6
     (B) -4
     (C) 8
     (D) 10
     (E) 12

GO ON TO THE NEXT PAGE

29. An ice cream parlor offers 5 flavors of ice cream with 7 different toppings in cups or cones. How many different combinations of 1 ice cream flavor, 1 topping, and either cup or cone can be chosen?

   (A) 14
   (B) 27
   (C) 35
   (D) 52
   (E) 70

30. Which equation has no real roots, but two complex roots?

   (A) $x^2 - 4x + 2$
   (B) $3x^2 + 10x - 1$
   (C) $4x^2 - 6x + 2$
   (D) $2x^2 - x + 6$
   (E) $x^2 - 2x - 8$

31. The slope of the linear function, f, is $-\frac{2}{3}$. If $f(-3) = 7$ and $f(6) = z$, what is z?

   (A) $-\frac{2}{3}$

   (B) $-\frac{1}{3}$

   (C) 1
   (D) 6
   (E) 10

32. Find the equation of a sphere whose center is at $(7, 4, -2)$ and passes through the origin?

   (A) $(x-2)^2 + (y-4)^2 + (z+7)^2 = 7$
   (B) $(x-7)^2 + (y-4)^2 + (z+2)^2 = 69$
   (C) $(x+7)^2 + (y+4)^2 + (z-2)^2 = 69$
   (D) $(x-2)^7 + (y-2)^4 + (z+2)^{-2} = 8$
   (E) $(x-7)^2 + (y-4)^2 + (z+2)^2 = 49$

33. The y-intercept of the line that passes through the points $(-1, 7)$ and $(2, -8)$ is

   (A) -5
   (B) -2
   (C) 2
   (D) 5
   (E) 6

34. Sixty people are at an audition for the school show. Twenty people are singers, 22 are actors, 30 are neither singers nor actors. How many people both sing and act?

   (A) 6
   (B) 8
   (C) 12
   (D) 14
   (E) 16

USE THIS SPACE AS SCRATCH PAPER

GO ON TO THE NEXT PAGE

35. The area of the triangle shown is
    (A) 44.8
    (B) 46.4
    (C) 82.9
    (D) 96.2
    (E) 119.4

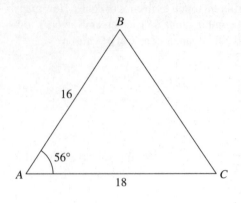

36. Which of the following lines are vertical asymptotes

    of the graph of $y = \dfrac{x^2}{x-3}$?

    I. $x = -3$
    II. $x = 0$
    III. $x = 3$

    (A) I only
    (B) II only
    (C) III only
    (D) I and III
    (E) II and III

37. What is the perimeter of the isosceles triangle below?

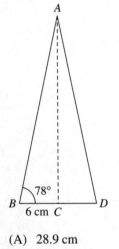

    (A) 28.9 cm
    (B) 57.2 cm
    (C) 69.7 cm
    (D) 78.6 cm
    (E) 86.6 cm

GO ON TO THE NEXT PAGE

38. If $f(x) = \sqrt{x}$ and $g(x) = 2x^2$, $(g \circ f)(x)$ equals

    (A) $\sqrt{2x}$
    (B) $4x^2$
    (C) $\dfrac{x^2}{2}$
    (D) $2x$
    (E) $x\sqrt{2}$

39. How many integers satisfy the inequality $x^2 + 10 < 7x$?

    (A) 0
    (B) 2
    (C) 3
    (D) 5
    (E) an infinite number

40. $\log_6 10 =$

    (A) 1.02
    (B) 1.29
    (C) 1.36
    (D) 1.59
    (E) 1.94

41. What is the mean value of the frequency distribution?

    (A) 3.0
    (B) 5.0
    (C) 6.5
    (D) 8.8
    (E) 20

Data Value	Frequency
5	4
6	6
7	8
8	3

42. What is the distance between the lines $3x - 4y = -7$ and $3x - 4y = -5$?

    (A) 0.25
    (B) 0.40
    (C) 0.72
    (D) 1.40
    (E) 1.96

43. $2x^5 - x^2 =$

    (A) x^3
    (B) $2x(1 - x^3)$
    (C) $x^2(2x^3 - 1)$
    (D) $\dfrac{2x^5}{x^2}$
    (E) $2x^3$

GO ON TO THE NEXT PAGE

44. If $f(x) = \dfrac{x-1}{x}$, then $f^{-1}(x)$ is

    (A) -1
    (B) $x^2 - x$
    (C) $\dfrac{x}{x-1}$
    (D) $\dfrac{-1}{x-1}$
    (E) $1 - \dfrac{1}{x+1}$

45. What are the coordinates of the vertex of the parabola whose equation is $y = 3x^2 + 18x + 9$?

    (A) $(1, -3)$
    (B) $(-3, 6)$
    (C) $(3, 18)$
    (D) $(-3, -18)$
    (E) $(18, -3)$

46. Which is the product of $(2 - i)(3 + 5i)$ in standard form?

    (A) $9 + 3i$
    (B) $10 + 2i$
    (C) $6 - 5i$
    (D) $1 + i$
    (E) $11 + 7i$

47. If point $P(3, 4)$ lies on the terminal side of $\angle\theta$ in standard position, $\cos\theta =$

    (A) $\dfrac{4}{5}$
    (B) $\dfrac{3}{4}$
    (C) $\dfrac{5}{3}$
    (D) $\dfrac{3}{5}$
    (E) $\dfrac{4}{3}$

48. Which of the following functions is even?

    I. $f(x) = 4x^3 - 2x$
    II. $f(x) = -x^2 + 6$
    III. $f(x) = |x| + 4$

    (A) I only
    (B) II only
    (C) III only
    (D) I and II
    (E) II and III

GO ON TO THE NEXT PAGE

49. $\sqrt[5]{3}\sqrt[3]{6}\sqrt[6]{2} =$

   (A) 1.8
   (B) 2.1
   (C) 2.5
   (D) 3.3
   (E) 6.0

50. A certain afterschool program has 50 students. Of those, 25 are involved in gymnastics, 35 are involved in basketball, and 14 do both. How many students do neither?

   (A) 2
   (B) 4
   (C) 7
   (D) 9
   (E) 12

USE THIS SPACE AS SCRATCH PAPER

S T O P

IF YOU FINISH BEFORE TIME IS CALLED, YOU MAY CHECK YOUR WORK ON THIS TEST ONLY.
DO NOT TURN TO ANY OTHER TEST IN THIS BOOK.

ANSWER KEY

1. C	11. E	21. B	31. C	41. C
2. C	12. B	22. A	32. B	42. B
3. A	13. D	23. C	33. C	43. C
4. B	14. C	24. D	34. C	44. D
5. D	15. E	25. A	35. E	45. D
6. E	16. E	26. A	36. C	46. E
7. D	17. B	27. C	37. C	47. D
8. E	18. E	28. D	38. D	48. E
9. B	19. B	29. E	39. B	49. C
10. D	20. E	30. D	40. B	50. B

ANSWERS AND EXPLANATIONS

1. **(C)** For the set to be a function, no x-values can be paired with more than one y-value. (4, 6) and (4, 13) violate this rule, so one must be removed. Only one is listed among the choices.

2. **(C)**

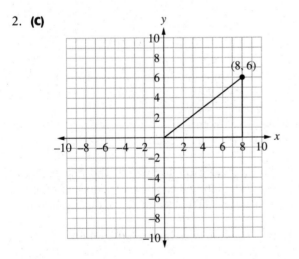

$r = \sqrt{x^2 + y^2} = \sqrt{8^2 + 6^2} = 10. \Theta = \tan^{-1}\left(\dfrac{y}{x}\right) = \tan^{-1}\left(\dfrac{6}{8}\right) = 36.87.$

3. **(A)** $f(-3) = x^2 + 3x - 1 = (-3)^2 + 3(-3) - 1 = 9 - 9 - 1 = -1.$

4. **(B)** Rewrite $f(x) = 8x + 2$ as $y = 8x + 2$. Then exchange the x and y to get $x = 8y + 2$ and solve to find that $y = \dfrac{x - 2}{8}$.

5. **(D)** The x-coordinate of the vertex is $x = -\dfrac{(-2)}{2(-1)} = -1$. The y-coordinate of the vertex is $6 - 2(-1) - (-1)^2 = 7$. Because $a < 0$, the parabola opens down. Therefore, $\{y: y \leq 7\}$.

6. **(E)**

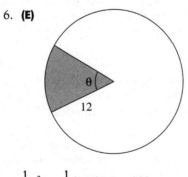

$A = \dfrac{1}{2}r^2\theta = \dfrac{1}{2}(144)2.5 \approx 180.$

7. **(D)** The sequence is geometric in which $n = 10$, $a_1 = 5$, and $r = 3$. The 10th term is $a_{10} = 5 \cdot 3^{10-1} = 98,415.$

8. **(E)** The sum of the zeros is $-\dfrac{b}{a} = -\dfrac{0}{5} = 0.$

9. **(B)** If $\sqrt{k} = 4.243$, then $k \approx 18$. So $10k = 180$, and $\sqrt{180} \approx 13.4$.

10. **(D)** Subtract the equations: $(5x + 3y) - (5x + 4y) = 34 - 32$, which becomes $x - y = 2$.

11. **(E)** Based on the diagram, $l = \dfrac{22}{\sin 45°}$ so $l = \dfrac{22}{\frac{\sqrt{2}}{2}} = \dfrac{44}{\sqrt{2}} = \dfrac{44\sqrt{2}}{2} = 22\sqrt{2}$.

12. **(B)** $f(2b + 1)$ directs you to replace x with $2b + 1$, and then simplify. Therefore, $f(2b + 1) = (2b + 1)^2 + 2(2b + 1) = 4b^2 + 4b + 1 + 4b + 2 = 4b^2 + 8b + 3$.

13. **(D)** Find $\dfrac{xy}{xz} = \dfrac{20}{30}$, which becomes $\dfrac{y}{z} = \dfrac{2}{3}$, so $z = \left(\dfrac{3}{2}\right)y$. Substitute this value into the third equation: $yz = 24$, so $y\left(\dfrac{3}{2}\right)y = 24$, which becomes $3y^2 = 48$ and $y = 4$. Therefore, $x = 5$ and $z = 6$, so the product is $5 \times 4 \times 6 = 120$.

14. **(C)** $\left|9^{-\frac{1}{2}} - 2(12^0)\right| = \left|\dfrac{1}{3} - 2\right| = \left|\dfrac{1}{3} - \dfrac{6}{3}\right| = \left|-\dfrac{5}{3}\right| = \dfrac{5}{3}$.

15. **(E)** Use the midpoint formula to find the center of the circle. $\left(\dfrac{0+4}{2}, \dfrac{3+3}{2}\right) = (2, 3)$. Then find half the length of the diameter to determine the radius: $d = \dfrac{1}{2}\sqrt{(4 - 0)^2 + (3 - 3)^2} = 2$. Insert the information into the standard equation for a circle: $(x - 2)^2 + (y - 3)^2 = 4$.

16. **(E)** Rewrite the equation in the form $y = 3x + 4$. The slope of the given line is 3. The slope of the line that is parallel is the same. Only choice E has a slope of 3.

17. **(B)** Rewrite $2 \log_6 x = \log_6 9$ as $\log_6 x^2 = \log_6 9$ by bringing the 2 into the log. Then cancel the logs because they have the same base, so $x^2 = 9$ and $x = 3$ or -3. However, -3 would be undefined, so $x = 3$.

18. **(E)** There are 36 elements in the sample space. Of those, 4 sums are equal to 9. Therefore, the probability is $\dfrac{4}{36}$ or $\dfrac{1}{9}$.

19. **(B)** Use the quadratic formula to find the roots $x = 1$ and -4. Therefore the sum is -3.

20. **(E)** According to the equation, $a = 6$ and $b = 5$. Find c: $c^2 = a^2 - b^2 = 36 - 25 = 11$, so $c = \sqrt{11}$. The ellipse is vertical, so the foci are at $(0, \sqrt{11})$ and $(0, -\sqrt{11})$.

21. **(B)** Enter cos 2nd cos 0.86 into your calculator set to degrees.

22. **(A)** The graph of the function $g(x)$ is stretched by a factor of a as $a\,g(x)$.

23. **(C)** Convert from radians to degrees: $\dfrac{\pi}{6}\left(\dfrac{180°}{\pi^R}\right) = \left(\dfrac{180\pi}{6\pi}\right)^R \approx 30°$.

24. **(D)** $x = 3 + 4i$, $ix = i(3 + 4i) = 3i + 4i^2 = 3i + 4(-1) = -4 + 3i$, which is d.

25. **(A)** Determine the values of x that would make the denominator zero. Factor to get $(x + 3)(x - 2) = 0$ so $x = -3$ or 2.

26. **(A)** Enter the values into the quadratic formula program on your graphing calculator, or test answers in function. Choose the positive zero and round to the nearest 10th.

27. **(C)** $\dfrac{180 + 152 + 165 + 170 + 205 + x}{6} = 175$, so $x = 178$.

28. **(D)** If $x + 4$ is a factor, it should divide into the polynomial without a remainder. Use synthetic division to solve:

-4	2	11	k	-8
		-8	-12	$-4k + 40$
	3	$k - 12$	$-4k + 40$	

Set the remainder equal to 0 and solve for k: $-4k + 40 = 0$, so $k = 10$.

29. **(E)** Use the multiplication principle to find that $5 \times 7 \times 2 = 70$.

30. **(D)** An equation for which the discriminant, $b^2 - 4ac$, is less than 0 has no real roots and two complex roots. Only (D) has a negative discriminant.

31. **(C)** The line goes through the points $(-3, 7)$ and $(6, z)$. Use the formula to find the slope and then use the given slope to solve for b: $m = \dfrac{z - 7}{6 - (-3)} = \dfrac{z - 7}{9}$ and $\dfrac{z - 7}{9} = -\dfrac{2}{3}$, so $z = 1$.

32. **(B)** Use the distance formula to calculate the radius: $d = \sqrt{(7 - 0)^2 + (4 - 0)^2 + (-2 - 0)^2} = \sqrt{69}$. Then use the results to describe the equation: $(x - 7)^2 + (y - 4)^2 + (z + 2)^2 = 69$.

33. **(C)** The slope of the line is $\dfrac{7-(-8)}{2-(-1)} = \dfrac{15}{3} = 5$. The point-slope equation is then $y - 7 = 5(x + 1)$. Solve for y to get $y = -5x + 2$. The y-intercept of the line is 2.

34. **(C)**

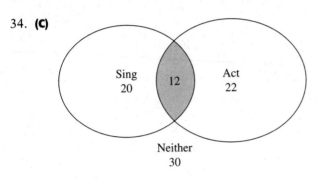

Neither
30

Use the formula $60 = 20 + 22 + 30 - x$, so $x = 12$.

35. **(E)** $a = \dfrac{1}{2}bc \cdot \sin A = \dfrac{1}{2}(16)(18)(0.829) \approx 119.4$.

36. **(C)** The vertical asymptotes are the nonremovable values of x that make the denominator zero. Set the denominator equal to zero and solve. $x - 3 = 0; x = 3$.

37. **(C)** Determine the length of AB. $\cos 78° = \dfrac{6}{AB}$, so $AB = \dfrac{6}{\cos 78°} = 28.86$. Therefore, the perimeter equals $28.86 + 28.86 + 12 = 69.7$ cm.

38. **(D)** $(g \circ f)(x) = g(f(x)) = g(\sqrt{x}) = 2(\sqrt{x})^2 = 2x$.

39. **(B)** $x^2 - 7x + 10 = (x - 2)(x - 5) = 0$ when $x = 2$ or 5. Integers between these values satisfy the inequality.

40. **(B)** Use the change-of-base formula to find $\dfrac{\log 10}{\log 6}$ by entering the values on your calculator.

41. **(C)** There are 21 data values. The mean is the sum of the data divided by the number of data values: $\dfrac{136}{21} = 6.5$.

42. **(B)** Rewrite the equations in simplest form. They become $3x - 4y + 7 = 0$ and $3x - 4y + 5 = 0$. The lines are parallel, so use the equation $d = \dfrac{|C_1 - C_2|}{\sqrt{A^2 + B^2}}$. Therefore, $d = \dfrac{|7 - 5|}{\sqrt{(3)^2 + (-4)^2}}$, which becomes $\dfrac{2}{5}$, or 0.4.

43. **(C)** Factor out the greatest common factor, which is x^2. Therefore, $2x^5 - x^2 = x^2(2x^3 - 1)$.

44. **(D)** Replace $f(x)$ with y. $f(x) = \dfrac{x-1}{x}$ becomes $y = \dfrac{x-1}{x}$. Then exchange x with y: $x = \dfrac{y-1}{y}$. Solve for y: $xy = y - 1; xy - y = -1; y(x - 1) = -1; y = \dfrac{-1}{x-1}$.

45. **(D)** The x-coordinate is $x = -\dfrac{b}{2a} = -\dfrac{18}{6} = -3$. The y-coordinate is $y = 3(-3)^2 + 18(-3) + 9 = -18$. Therefore, the vertex occurs at the point $(-3, -18)$.

46. **(E)** The fastest method is to enter the problem into your calculator. Use 2nd decimal to enter i. Alternatively, you can use the foil method to multiply and remember to replace i^2 with -1.

$(2 - i)(3 + 5i)$
$6 + 10i - 3i - 5i^2$
$6 + 7i + 5$
$11 + 7i$

47. **(D)** It is most useful to draw a diagram to solve the problem.

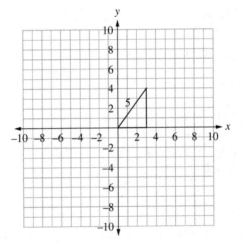

Use the Pythagorean Theorem to calculate the length of the hypotenuse as 5. Therefore, $\cos \theta = \dfrac{3}{5}$.

48. **(E)** Check each function for $-x$: For $f(x) = 4x^3 - 2x$, $f(-x) = 4(-x)^3 - 2(-x) = -4x + 2$. The signs are opposite to the original function, so the function is odd. For $f(x) = -x^2 + 6$, $f(-x) = -(-x)^2 + 6 = -(x)^2 + 6$. The final expression is the same as the original, so the function is even. For, $|x| + 4$, $|-x| + 4 = |x| + 4$, so the function is even.

49. **(C)** $3^{\frac{1}{5}}6^{\frac{1}{3}}2^{\frac{1}{6}} \approx 2.5$.

50. **(B)** Add $25 + 35$, and then subtract the 14 who are counted twice. Therefore, 46 students are involved in gymnastics, basketball, or both. The remaining students $(50 - 46)$ do neither.

▬ DIAGNOSE YOUR STRENGTHS AND WEAKNESSES

Check the number of each question answered correctly and "X" the number of each question answered incorrectly.

Algebra and Functions	1	3	4	5	8	9	10	12	13	14	16	17	19	25		Total Number Correct
29 questions																
	26	28	30	31	33	36	38	39	40	42	43	44	45	48	49	

Trigonometry	6	11	21	23	35	37	47	Total Number Correct
7 questions								

Coordinate and Three-Dimensional Geometry	2	15	20	22	32	Total Number Correct
5 questions						

Numbers and Operations	7	24	29	46	50	Total Number Correct
5 questions						

Data Analysis, Statistics, and Probability	18	27	34	41	Total Number Correct
4 questions					

Number of correct answers $-\dfrac{1}{4}$ **(Number of incorrect answers) = Your raw score**

$$\underline{\hspace{4cm}} - \frac{1}{4} \left(\underline{\hspace{4cm}} \right) = \underline{\hspace{3cm}}$$

Compare your raw score with the approximate SAT Subject Test score below:

	Raw Score	SAT Subject Test Approximate Score
Excellent	43–50	770–800
Very Good	33–43	670–770
Good	27–33	620–670
Above Average	21–27	570–620
Average	11–21	500–570
Below Average	< 11	< 500

PRACTICE TEST 10

Treat this practice test as the actual test and complete it in one 60-minute sitting. Use the following answer sheet to fill in your multiple-choice answers. Once you have completed the practice test:

1. Check your answers using the Answer Key.
2. Review the Answers and Solutions.
3. Fill in the "Diagnose Your Strengths and Weaknesses" sheet, and determine areas that require further preparation.

PRACTICE TEST 10

MATH LEVEL 2

ANSWER SHEET

Tear out this answer sheet and use it to complete the practice test. Determine the BEST answer for each question. Then, fill in the appropriate oval using a No. 2 pencil.

1. Ⓐ Ⓑ Ⓒ Ⓓ Ⓔ	21. Ⓐ Ⓑ Ⓒ Ⓓ Ⓔ	41. Ⓐ Ⓑ Ⓒ Ⓓ Ⓔ
2. Ⓐ Ⓑ Ⓒ Ⓓ Ⓔ	22. Ⓐ Ⓑ Ⓒ Ⓓ Ⓔ	42. Ⓐ Ⓑ Ⓒ Ⓓ Ⓔ
3. Ⓐ Ⓑ Ⓒ Ⓓ Ⓔ	23. Ⓐ Ⓑ Ⓒ Ⓓ Ⓔ	43. Ⓐ Ⓑ Ⓒ Ⓓ Ⓔ
4. Ⓐ Ⓑ Ⓒ Ⓓ Ⓔ	24. Ⓐ Ⓑ Ⓒ Ⓓ Ⓔ	44. Ⓐ Ⓑ Ⓒ Ⓓ Ⓔ
5. Ⓐ Ⓑ Ⓒ Ⓓ Ⓔ	25. Ⓐ Ⓑ Ⓒ Ⓓ Ⓔ	45. Ⓐ Ⓑ Ⓒ Ⓓ Ⓔ
6. Ⓐ Ⓑ Ⓒ Ⓓ Ⓔ	26. Ⓐ Ⓑ Ⓒ Ⓓ Ⓔ	46. Ⓐ Ⓑ Ⓒ Ⓓ Ⓔ
7. Ⓐ Ⓑ Ⓒ Ⓓ Ⓔ	27. Ⓐ Ⓑ Ⓒ Ⓓ Ⓔ	47. Ⓐ Ⓑ Ⓒ Ⓓ Ⓔ
8. Ⓐ Ⓑ Ⓒ Ⓓ Ⓔ	28. Ⓐ Ⓑ Ⓒ Ⓓ Ⓔ	48. Ⓐ Ⓑ Ⓒ Ⓓ Ⓔ
9. Ⓐ Ⓑ Ⓒ Ⓓ Ⓔ	29. Ⓐ Ⓑ Ⓒ Ⓓ Ⓔ	49. Ⓐ Ⓑ Ⓒ Ⓓ Ⓔ
10. Ⓐ Ⓑ Ⓒ Ⓓ Ⓔ	30. Ⓐ Ⓑ Ⓒ Ⓓ Ⓔ	50. Ⓐ Ⓑ Ⓒ Ⓓ Ⓔ
11. Ⓐ Ⓑ Ⓒ Ⓓ Ⓔ	31. Ⓐ Ⓑ Ⓒ Ⓓ Ⓔ	
12. Ⓐ Ⓑ Ⓒ Ⓓ Ⓔ	32. Ⓐ Ⓑ Ⓒ Ⓓ Ⓔ	
13. Ⓐ Ⓑ Ⓒ Ⓓ Ⓔ	33. Ⓐ Ⓑ Ⓒ Ⓓ Ⓔ	
14. Ⓐ Ⓑ Ⓒ Ⓓ Ⓔ	34. Ⓐ Ⓑ Ⓒ Ⓓ Ⓔ	
15. Ⓐ Ⓑ Ⓒ Ⓓ Ⓔ	35. Ⓐ Ⓑ Ⓒ Ⓓ Ⓔ	
16. Ⓐ Ⓑ Ⓒ Ⓓ Ⓔ	36. Ⓐ Ⓑ Ⓒ Ⓓ Ⓔ	
17. Ⓐ Ⓑ Ⓒ Ⓓ Ⓔ	37. Ⓐ Ⓑ Ⓒ Ⓓ Ⓔ	
18. Ⓐ Ⓑ Ⓒ Ⓓ Ⓔ	38. Ⓐ Ⓑ Ⓒ Ⓓ Ⓔ	
19. Ⓐ Ⓑ Ⓒ Ⓓ Ⓔ	39. Ⓐ Ⓑ Ⓒ Ⓓ Ⓔ	
20. Ⓐ Ⓑ Ⓒ Ⓓ Ⓔ	40. Ⓐ Ⓑ Ⓒ Ⓓ Ⓔ	

PRACTICE TEST 10

Time: 60 minutes

Directions: Select the BEST answer for each of the 50 multiple-choice questions. If the exact solution is not one of the five choices, select the answer that is the best approximation. Then, fill in the appropriate oval on the answer sheet.

Notes:

1. A calculator will be needed to answer some of the questions on the test. Scientific, programmable, and graphing calculators are permitted. It is up to you to determine when and when not to use your calculator.
2. Angles on the Level 2 test are measured in degrees and radians. You need to decide whether your calculator should be set to degree mode or radian mode for a particular question.
3. Figures are drawn as accurately as possible and are intended to help solve some of the test problems. If a figure is not drawn to scale, this will be stated in the problem. All figures lie in a plane unless the problem indicates otherwise.
4. Unless otherwise stated, the domain of a function f is assumed to be the set of real numbers x for which the value of the function, $f(x)$, is a real number.
5. Reference information that may be useful in answering some of the test questions can be found below.

Reference Information	
Right circular cone with radius r and height h:	Volume $= \dfrac{1}{3}\pi r^2 h$
Right circular cone with circumference of base c and slant height ℓ:	Lateral Area $= \dfrac{1}{2}c\ell$
Sphere with radius r:	Volume $= \dfrac{4}{3}\pi r^3$ Surface Area $= 4\pi r^2$
Pyramid with base area B and height h:	Volume $= \dfrac{1}{3}Bh$

PRACTICE TEST 10 QUESTIONS

1. $f(x) = ax$ and $g(x) = 2bx$. If $f(g(x)) = 2x^2 - 6$, what is ab?

   (A) $x - \dfrac{3}{x}$

   (B) $3 - \dfrac{1}{x}$

   (C) $1 - \dfrac{3}{x}$

   (D) $\dfrac{1}{2} + \dfrac{3}{x}$

   (E) $\dfrac{3}{2} + x$

2. A point has polar coordinates (4, 40°). The same point can be also be represented as

   (A) (3.06, 2.57)
   (B) (0.99, 0.64)
   (C) (2.57, 3.06)
   (D) (6.00, 6.32)
   (E) (39.9, 2.79)

3. Which of the following is a transformation that shifts $f(x)$ two units to the right and one unit upward?

   (A) $f(2x - 1)$
   (B) $f(x - 2) + 1$
   (C) $\dfrac{1}{2} f(x)$
   (D) $f(x - 1) + 2$
   (E) $f\left(x + \dfrac{1}{2}\right)$

4. If $f(x) = 3x^2 + 2x + 1$, then $f(b + 2) =$

   (A) $3b^2 + 10b + 2$
   (B) $2b^2 + 6b + 13$
   (C) $b^2 + 14b + 4$
   (D) $b^2 + 12b + 12$
   (E) $3b^2 + 14b + 17$

5. 28 radians is equivalent to

   (A) 49°
   (B) 88°
   (C) 504°
   (D) 1008°
   (E) 1605°

GO ON TO THE NEXT PAGE

6. If $x - 1$ and $2x + 2$ are factors of $2x^3 + 6x^2 - 2x - b$, then b must be

   (A) −2
   (B) 2
   (C) 6
   (D) 8
   (E) 10

7. A teacher is selecting groups of 3 students. How many different groups can be selected from a class of 22 students?

   (A) 250
   (B) 660
   (C) 969
   (D) 1540
   (E) 2230

8. Which of the following is parallel to the line $y + \dfrac{1}{3}x = 5$?

   (A) $y = \dfrac{3}{5}x + 1$

   (B) $y = -\dfrac{1}{3}x + 10$

   (C) $y = -3x - 1$

   (D) $y = \dfrac{1}{3}x + 3$

   (E) $y = 3x - 5$

9. If the triangle below is rotated 360° about the axis AB, what is the surface area of the resulting solid?

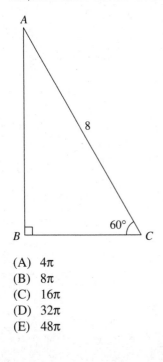

   (A) 4π
   (B) 8π
   (C) 16π
   (D) 32π
   (E) 48π

GO ON TO THE NEXT PAGE

10. Which is the equation of a circle that has a diameter with endpoints at $A(1, 4)$ and $B(1, 0)$?

    (A) $(x - 1)^2 + (y - 4)^2 = 1$
    (B) $(x + 2)^2 + (y - 1)^2 = 2$
    (C) $(x - 1)^2 + (y - 2)^2 = 4$
    (D) $(x + 1)^2 + (y + 2)^2 = 2$
    (E) $(x - 2)^2 + (y + 1)^2 = 4$

11. If $\log_3 x = -2$, what is the value of x?

    (A) -6
    (B) $\dfrac{1}{9}$
    (C) $\dfrac{1}{3}$
    (D) $\dfrac{1}{2}$
    (E) 6

12. What is the median value of the frequency distribution?

    (A) 3
    (B) 12
    (C) 18
    (D) 20
    (E) 28

Data Value	Frequency
16	2
17	9
18	12
19	5

13. Which of the following functions is even?

    I. $f(x) = x^2 + 2$
    II. $f(x) = \cos x$
    III. $f(x) = \sin x$

    (A) I only
    (B) II only
    (C) III only
    (D) I and II
    (E) II and III

14. What is the number of radians in $\cot^{-1}(-3.2146)$?

    (A) -0.3
    (B) -1.3
    (C) -3.2
    (D) -17.3
    (E) none of these

GO ON TO THE NEXT PAGE

15. If $\dfrac{2x+2y}{x} = 8$, what is the value of $\dfrac{x}{y}$?

    (A) $\dfrac{1}{6}$

    (B) $\dfrac{1}{3}$

    (C) $\dfrac{1}{4}$

    (D) $\dfrac{2}{3}$

    (E) $\dfrac{3}{8}$

16. How many integers satisfy the inequality $x^2 - 3 < 2x$?

    (A) 0
    (B) 2
    (C) 3
    (D) 5
    (E) an infinite number

17. $\log_8 \sqrt{24} - \log_8 \sqrt{6} =$

    (A) $\dfrac{1}{3}$

    (B) $\dfrac{1}{2}$

    (C) $\dfrac{2}{4}$

    (D) 6
    (E) 8

18. If $2x^{\frac{3}{2}} = 6$, then $x =$

    (A) 1.5
    (B) 2.0
    (C) 2.1
    (D) 4.0
    (E) 5.2

19. If $\log_a(x+4) = \log_a x + \log_a 9$, then the value of x is

    (A) $\dfrac{4}{9}$

    (B) $\dfrac{1}{2}$

    (C) $\dfrac{5}{4}$

    (D) 5
    (E) 13

USE THIS SPACE AS SCRATCH PAPER

GO ON TO THE NEXT PAGE

20. If a circle has a circumference of 20 inches, the area of a sector with a central angle of $\dfrac{2\pi}{3}$ radians to the nearest whole number is

    (A) 3
    (B) 11
    (C) 21
    (D) 33
    (E) 42

21. If $\log_x(2) = 0.3869$ and $\log_x(3) = 0.6131$, what is $\log_x(6)$?

    (A) 0.2262
    (B) 0.2372
    (C) 0.5000
    (D) 1.000
    (E) 1.2851

22. Which point is a focus of the ellipse whose equation is $\dfrac{x^2}{4} + \dfrac{y^2}{9} = 1$?

    (A) $(0, \sqrt{5})$
    (B) $(3, 0)$
    (C) $(0, -\sqrt{13})$
    (D) $(\sqrt{5}, 3)$
    (E) $(0, -9)$

23. The slope of the linear function, f, is 3. If $f(2) = 2$ and $f(3) = z$, what is z?

    (A) −3
    (B) −1
    (C) 1
    (D) 5
    (E) 6

24. What is the radius of a sphere with the center at the origin that passes through the point $(-2, -3, 4)$?

    (A) 1.73
    (B) 2.90
    (C) 3.00
    (D) 4.26
    (E) 5.39

25. The y-intercept of the line that passes through the points $(-3, 0)$ and $(-1, -2)$ is

    (A) −3
    (B) −1
    (C) 1
    (D) 4
    (E) 6

26. $2x^{\frac{1}{5}} + x^{\frac{3}{5}} =$

 (A) $2x^{\frac{2}{5}}$

 (B) $3x^{\frac{4}{5}}$

 (C) $x^{\frac{1}{5}}(2 + x^{\frac{2}{5}})$

 (D) $x^{\frac{1}{5}}(x^{\frac{3}{5}})$

 (E) $3x^{\frac{3}{25}}$

27. Two dice are thrown. What is the probability of getting a sum of 3 or 7?

 (A) $\dfrac{1}{2}$

 (B) $\dfrac{2}{9}$

 (C) $\dfrac{1}{6}$

 (D) $\dfrac{3}{8}$

 (E) $\dfrac{1}{9}$

28. If point $P(-5, -12)$ lies on the terminal side of $\angle\theta$ in standard position, $\sin\theta =$

 (A) $\dfrac{5}{12}$

 (B) $\dfrac{13}{5}$

 (C) $\dfrac{5}{-13}$

 (D) $\dfrac{-12}{5}$

 (E) $\dfrac{12}{-13}$

29. If $\sin x = \dfrac{2}{3}$, $\cos 2x =$

 (A) $\dfrac{1}{9}$

 (B) $\dfrac{8}{9}$

 (C) $\dfrac{4}{3}$

 (D) $\dfrac{1}{2}$

 (E) $\dfrac{3}{2}$

GO ON TO THE NEXT PAGE

30. Which is the modulus of $3 + 2i$?

    (A) $\sqrt{5}$
    (B) $\sqrt{10}$
    (C) $\sqrt{13}$
    (D) 5
    (E) 6

31. Which of the following lines are vertical asymptotes of the graph of $y = \dfrac{x+2}{x^2-16}$?

    I. $x = -4$
    II. $x = -2$
    III. $x = 4$

    (A) I only
    (B) II only
    (C) III only
    (D) I and III
    (E) II and III

32. If $f(x) = 4x + 8$, then $f^{-1}(x)$ is

    (A) $4x - 8$
    (B) $\dfrac{x}{4} - 2$
    (C) $\dfrac{1}{4x+8}$
    (D) $x + 4$
    (E) $x^2 + 64$

33. If $3x + 2y = 4$ and $2x + y = 3$, what is $x + y$?

    (A) −1
    (B) 0
    (C) 1
    (D) 7
    (E) 12

34. A gumball machine has 10 blue, 9 white, 12 green, 20 red, and 8 yellow. Marisol likes only white gumballs. If a gumball comes out of the machine at random, what is the probability that she will get a white gumball?

    (A) 0.15
    (B) 0.43
    (C) 0.50
    (D) 0.86
    (E) 0.90

35. The 10th term of the arithmetic sequence 3, 7, 11, 15, … is

    (A) 31
    (B) 33
    (C) 36
    (D) 39
    (E) 41

GO ON TO THE NEXT PAGE

36. To the nearest 10th, the positive zero of $y = 2x^2 + 8x - 6$ is

    (A) 0.6
    (B) 0.9
    (C) 1.7
    (D) 3.2
    (E) 4.6

USE THIS SPACE AS SCRATCH PAPER

37. What is the distance between the lines $-3x + 4y = -2$ and $-3x + 4y = 1$?

    (A) 0.2
    (B) 0.4
    (C) 0.6
    (D) 1.4
    (E) 1.7

38. How many integers satisfy the inequality $x^2 + 3x < 4$?

    (A) 0
    (B) 1
    (C) 3
    (D) 4
    (E) an infinite number

39. If $\sqrt{k} = 2.646$, then $\sqrt{10k} =$

    (A) 6.5
    (B) 8.4
    (C) 70.6
    (D) 179.6
    (E) 264.6

40. If $x - 5$ is a factor of $3x^3 - 13x^2 - kx + 20$, what is the value of k?

    (A) −4
    (B) −3
    (C) 9
    (D) 11
    (E) 14

41. Which data set has the greatest standard deviation?

    (A) {8, 8, 8}
    (B) {2, 8, 14}
    (C) {6, 8, 10}
    (D) {4, 8, 12}
    (E) {7, 8, 9}

42. If $f(x) = 2x + 3$ and $g(x) = 4x$, $(f + g)(x)$ equals

    (A) $6x + 3$
    (B) $6x^2$
    (C) $2x + 1$
    (D) $2x$
    (E) $2x^2 + 2$

GO ON TO THE NEXT PAGE

43. $\log_4 9 =$

    (A) 1.21
    (B) 1.29
    (C) 1.36
    (D) 1.58
    (E) 1.63

44. In the triangle below, what is the value of b to the nearest whole number?

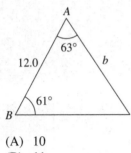

    (A) 10
    (B) 11
    (C) 12
    (D) 13
    (E) 14

45. What is the domain of $f(x) = \sqrt{2x - 2}$?

    (A) $\{x : x \neq -2 \text{ or } 2\}$
    (B) $\{x : x \geq 0\}$
    (C) $\{x : x < -2\}$
    (D) $\{x : x \geq 1\}$
    (E) all real numbers

46. What are the coordinates of the vertex of the parabola whose equation is $y = 5x^2 + 10x + 1$?

    (A) $(-1, -4)$
    (B) $(-1, 5)$
    (C) $(5, 10)$
    (D) $(1, -10)$
    (E) $(16, -8)$

47. A student needs an average of 92 on 3 exams to be considered for scholarship. The student scored 94 on the first exam. What is the lowest score the student can get on the remaining exams and still be considered for the scholarship?

    (A) 82
    (B) 88
    (C) 90
    (D) 92
    (E) 96

GO ON TO THE NEXT PAGE

48. If $A = \begin{pmatrix} -2 & 3 \\ 1 & 0 \end{pmatrix}$ and $B = \begin{pmatrix} 4 & -1 \\ 3 & 2 \end{pmatrix}$, then AB is

(A) $\begin{pmatrix} 2 & 2 \\ 4 & 3 \end{pmatrix}$

(B) $\begin{pmatrix} -6 & -1 \\ -2 & -2 \end{pmatrix}$

(C) $\begin{pmatrix} -8 & -3 \\ 3 & 0 \end{pmatrix}$

(D) $\begin{pmatrix} 2 & -3 \\ 1 & 2 \end{pmatrix}$

(E) $\begin{pmatrix} 1 & 8 \\ 4 & -1 \end{pmatrix}$

49. The area of the triangle shown is
(A) 28.1
(B) 33.5
(C) 58.9
(D) 66.9
(E) 117.7

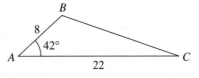

50. Which is the product of $(4 + 6i)(1 - 3i)$ in standard form?

(A) $22 - 6i$
(B) $24 + 3i$
(C) $12 - 4i$
(D) $1 + i$
(E) $9 + 2i$

S T O P

IF YOU FINISH BEFORE TIME IS CALLED, YOU MAY CHECK YOUR WORK ON THIS TEST ONLY.
DO NOT TURN TO ANY OTHER TEST IN THIS BOOK.

ANSWER KEY

1. A	11. B	21. D	31. D	41. B
2. A	12. C	22. A	32. B	42. A
3. B	13. D	23. D	33. C	43. D
4. E	14. A	24. E	34. A	44. D
5. E	15. B	25. A	35. D	45. D
6. C	16. C	26. C	36. A	46. A
7. D	17. B	27. B	37. C	47. A
8. B	18. C	28. E	38. D	48. E
9. E	19. B	29. A	39. B	49. C
10. C	20. B	30. C	40. E	50. A

ANSWERS AND EXPLANATIONS

1. **(A)** $f(g(x)) = f(2bx) = 2abx$. Therefore, $2abx = 2x^2 - 6$. Factor, $2x$ out of the right side: $2abx = 2x\left(x - \dfrac{3}{x}\right)$, so $ab = x - \dfrac{3}{x}$.

2. **(A)** Sketch a diagram to visualize the relationship between polar coordinates and rectangular coordinates.

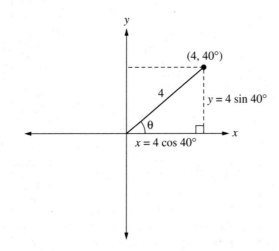

Then calculate each coordinate.

3. **(B)** Shifting 2 units to the right requires subtracting 2 before the function is applied. Shifting 1 unit upward requires adding 1 after the function is applied.

4. **(E)** $f(b + 2)$ directs you to replace x with $b + 2$, and then simplify. Therefore, $f(b + 2) = 3(b + 2)^2 + 2(b + 2) + 1 = 3(b^2 + 4b + 4) + 2b + 4 + 1 = 3b^2 + 14b + 17$.

5. **(E)** Convert from radians to degrees: $28\left(\dfrac{180°}{\pi^R}\right) = \left(\dfrac{5040}{\pi}\right)^R \approx 1605°$.

6. **(C)** If $x - 1$ is a factor, $P(1) = 2(1)^3 + 6(1)^2 - 2(1) - b = 0$, so $b = 6$.

7. **(D)** Determine the number of ways 3 objects can be selected from 22, or $\dbinom{22}{3} = 1540$.

8. **(B)** Rewrite the equation in the form $y = -\dfrac{1}{3}x + 5$. The slope of the given line is $-\dfrac{1}{3}$. The slope of the line that is parallel is the same.

9. **(E)** Sketch the resulting solid.

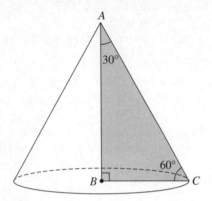

The lateral height of the cone is the hypotenuse of the triangle, which is 8. The radius is equal to the length of BC. $\sin 30 = \dfrac{BC}{8}$, $BC = 8 \sin 30 = 4$. Now substitute the values into the formula for the surface area of a cone: $SA = \pi r^2 + \pi r l = \pi(4)^2 + \pi(4)(8) = 16\pi + 32\pi = 48\pi$.

10. **(C)** Use the midpoint formula to find the center of the circle. $\left(\dfrac{1+1}{2}, \dfrac{4+0}{2}\right) = (1, 2)$. Then find half the length of the diameter to determine the radius: $d = \dfrac{1}{2}\sqrt{(1-1)^2 + (4-0)^2} = 2$. Insert the information into the standard equation for a circle: $(x - 1)^2 + (y - 2)^2 = 4$.

11. **(B)** The equation $\log_3 x = -2$ is equivalent to $3^{-2} = x$. Therefore, $x = \dfrac{1}{9}$.

12. **(C)** There are 28 data values. The median is the mean of the 14th and 15th largest values. They are both 18, so the median is 18.

13. **(D)** A function is even if $f(x) = f(-x)$ for all values of x. Therefore, there is symmetry about the y-axis. This is true for functions I and II only.

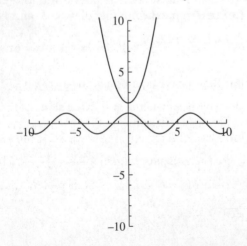

A function is odd if $-f(x) = f(-x)$ for all values of x. Function III is odd. It is symmetric about the origin.

14. **(A)** Set your calculator in radian mode. Then enter 2nd tan $\left(\dfrac{1}{-3.2146}\right)$.

15. **(B)** Multiply through by x to get $2x + 2y = 8x$. Subtract $2x$ from both sides to get $2y = 6x$. Divide both sides by $6y$ to find that $\dfrac{x}{y} = \dfrac{1}{3}$.

16. **(C)** $x^2 - 2x - 3 = (x - 3)(x + 1) = 0$ when $x = 3$ or -1. Numbers between these values satisfy the inequality.

17. **(B)** $\log_8 \sqrt{24} - \log_8 \sqrt{6} = \log_8 \dfrac{\sqrt{24}}{\sqrt{6}} = \log_8 \sqrt{4} = \log_8 2$. Rewrite as $\log_8 2 = x$ so $8^x = 2$ and $(2^3)^x = 2$. Therefore, $2^{3x} = 2^1$ and $x = \dfrac{1}{3}$.

18. **(C)** Divide the equation by 2 to get $x^{\frac{3}{2}} = 3$. Then raise both sides to the power of $\dfrac{2}{3}$: $x = 3^{\frac{2}{3}} \approx 2.1$.

19. **(B)** Use the properties of logarithms to rewrite $\log_a x + \log_a 9$ as $\log_a (9x)$. That means that $\log_a (x + 4) = \log_a (9x)$. This is true when $x + 4 = 9x$, so $x = \dfrac{1}{2}$.

20. **(B)** First find the radius of the circle: $C = 2\pi r$, so $20 = 2\pi r$ and $r \approx 3.18$. Then use the radius to calculate the area: $A = \dfrac{1}{2}r^2\theta = \dfrac{1}{2}(3.18)^2\dfrac{2\pi}{3} \approx 10.58$.

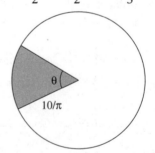

21. **(D)** Because $2 \times 3 = 6$, use the properties of logarithms to rewrite as $\log_x(6) = \log_x(2 \cdot 3) = \log_x(2) + \log_x(3) = 0.3869 + 0.6131 = 1.0000$.

22. **(A)** According to the equation, $a = 3$ and $b = 2$. Find c: $c^2 = a^2 - b^2 = 9 - 4 = 5$, so $c = \sqrt{5}$. The ellipse is vertical, so the foci are at $(0, \sqrt{5})$ and $(0, -\sqrt{5})$.

23. **(D)** The line goes through the points $(2, 2)$ and $(3, z)$. Use the formula to find the slope and then use the given slope to solve for b: $m = \dfrac{z - 2}{3 - 2} = \dfrac{z - 2}{1}$ and $z - 2 = 3$ so $z = 5$.

24. **(E)** Use the distance formula to find the radius of the sphere: $d = \sqrt{(-2-0)^2 + (-3-0)^2 + (4-0)^2} = \sqrt{29}$. Use your calculator to find that $r \approx 5.39$.

25. **(A)** The slope of the line is $\dfrac{0-(-2)}{-3-(-1)} = \dfrac{2}{-2} = -1$. The point-slope equation is then $y - 0 = -(x+3)$. Solve for y to get $y = -x - 3$. The y-intercept of the line is -3.

26. **(C)** Factor out the greatest common factor, which is $x^{\frac{1}{5}}$. Therefore, $2x^{\frac{1}{5}} + x^{\frac{3}{5}} = x^{\frac{1}{5}}(2 + x^{\frac{2}{5}})$.

27. **(B)** $P(3) = \dfrac{2}{36}$ and $P(7) = \dfrac{6}{36}$. $P(A \cup B) = \dfrac{2}{36} + \dfrac{6}{36} = \dfrac{8}{36} = \dfrac{2}{9}$.

28. **(E)** It is most useful to draw a diagram to solve the problem.

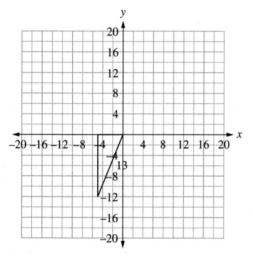

Use the Pythagorean Theorem to calculate the length of the hypotenuse as 13. Therefore, $\sin \theta = \dfrac{-12}{13}$.

29. **(A)** Use the identity $\cos 2x = 1 - 2\sin^2 x = 1 - 2\left(\dfrac{4}{9}\right) = \dfrac{1}{9}$.

30. **(C)** The real and imaginary parts of the complex number are 3 and 2. Therefore, the modulus is $\sqrt{3^2 + 2^2} = \sqrt{13}$.

31. **(D)** The vertical asymptotes are the nonremovable values of x that make the denominator zero. Set the denominator equal to zero and solve; $x^2 - 16 = 0$, so $x = -4$ and 4.

32. **(B)** Replace $f(x)$ with y. $f(x) = 4x + 8$ becomes $y = 4x + 8$. Then exchange x and y: $x = 4y + 8$. Solve for y: $x - 8 = 4y$; $\dfrac{x}{4} - \dfrac{8}{4} = y$; $\dfrac{x}{4} - 2 = y$.

33. **(C)** Subtract the equations: $(3x + 2y) - (2x + y) = 4 - 3$, which becomes $x + y = 1$.

34. **(A)** There are a total of 59 gumballs, 9 of which are white. P(white) $= \dfrac{9}{59} = 0.15$.

35. **(D)** $a_n = a_1 + (n-1)d$, so $a_{10} = 3 + (10-1)4 = 39$.

36. **(A)** Enter the values into the quadratic formula program on your graphing calculator, or test answers in function. Choose the positive zero and round to the nearest 10th.

37. **(C)** Rewrite the equations in simplest form. They become $-3x + 4y + 2 = 0$ and $-3x + 4y - 1 = 0$. The lines are parallel, so use the equation $d = \dfrac{|C_1 - C_2|}{\sqrt{A^2 + B^2}}$. Therefore, $d = \dfrac{|2 - (-1)|}{\sqrt{(-3)^2 + (4)^2}}$, which becomes $\dfrac{3}{5}$, or 0.6.

38. **(D)** $x^2 + 3x - 4 = (x+4)(x-1) = 0$ when $x = -4$ or 1. Integers between these values satisfy the inequality.

39. **(B)** If $\sqrt{k} = 2.646$, then $k \approx 7$. So $10k = 70$, and $\sqrt{70} \approx 8.4$.

40. **(E)** If $x - 5$ is a factor, it should divide into the polynomial without a remainder. Use synthetic division to solve:

5	3	−13	−k	20
		15	10	−5k + 50
	2	−k + 10	−5k + 70

Set the remainder equal to 0 and solve for k: $-5k + 70 = 0$, so $k = 14$.

41. **(B)** The mean of all the data sets is 8. The data set with the greatest standard deviation, therefore, has the greatest spread.

42. **(A)** $(f + g)(x) = f(x) + g(x) = 2x + 3 + 4x = 6x + 3$.

43. **(D)** Use the change-of-base formula to find $\dfrac{\log 9}{\log 4}$ by entering the values on your calculator.

44. **(D)** First, find the missing angle $\angle C = 180 - (61 + 63) = 56°$. Then, use sin ratios: $\dfrac{\sin 56}{12} = \dfrac{\sin 61}{b}$. Therefore, $12 \sin 61° = b \sin 56°$, which means that $b = \dfrac{12 \sin 61°}{\sin 56°} = 13$.

45. **(D)** Determine the values of x that would make the radicand negative. $2x - 2 \geq 0$ so $x \geq 1$

46. **(A)** The x-coordinate is $x = -\dfrac{b}{2a} = -\dfrac{10}{10} = -1$. The y-coordinate is $y = 5(1)^2 + 10(-1) + 1 = -4$. Therefore, the vertex occurs at the point $(1, -4)$.

47. **(A)** The scores are averages, so $3 \cdot 92 = 276$. The student already scored 94, so $276 - 94 = 182$. The highest score the student can earn is 100, so the lowest score the student can get is $182 - 100 = 82$.

48. **(E)** $\begin{pmatrix} -2 & 3 \\ 1 & 0 \end{pmatrix} \begin{pmatrix} 4 & -1 \\ 3 & 2 \end{pmatrix} =$

$\begin{pmatrix} (-2 \cdot 4) + (3 \cdot 3) & (-2 \cdot -1) + (3 \cdot 2) \\ (1 \cdot 4) + (0 \cdot 3) & (1 \cdot -1) + (0 \cdot 2) \end{pmatrix}$ You can also use the matrix function on your calculator.

49. **(C)** $a = \dfrac{1}{2}bc \cdot \sin A = \dfrac{1}{2}(8)(22)(0.669) \approx 58.9$.

50. **(A)** The fastest method is to enter the problem into your calculator. Use 2nd decimal to enter i. Alternatively, you can use the foil method to multiply and remember to replace i^2 with -1.

$(4 + 6i)(1 - 3i)$

$4 - 12i + 6i - 18i^2$

$4 - 6i + 18$

$22 - 6i$

▮▮▮ DIAGNOSE YOUR STRENGTHS AND WEAKNESSES

Check the number of each question answered correctly and "X" the number of each question answered incorrectly.

Algebra and Functions	1	4	6	8	11	13	15	16	17	18	19	21	23	25	Total Number Correct
27 questions															
	26	31	32	33	36	37	38	39	40	42	43	45	46		

Trigonometry	5	9	14	20	28	29	44	49	Total Number Correct
8 questions									

Coordinate and Three-Dimensional Geometry	2	3	10	22	24	Total Number Correct
5 questions						

Numbers and Operations	7	30	35	48	50	Total Number Correct
5 questions						

Data Analysis, Statistics, and Probability	12	27	34	41	47	Total Number Correct
5 questions						

Number of correct answers $-\dfrac{1}{4}$ **(Number of incorrect answers) = Your raw score**

_____ $-\dfrac{1}{4}$ (_____) = _____

Compare your raw score with the approximate SAT Subject Test score below:

	Raw Score	SAT Subject Test Approximate Score
Excellent	43–50	770–800
Very Good	33–43	670–770
Good	27–33	620–670
Above Average	21–27	570–620
Average	11–21	500–570
Below Average	< 11	< 500